TWAYNE'S WORLD LEADERS SERIES

EDITORS OF THIS VOLUME

Arthur W. Brown

Baruch College, The City University

of New York

and

Thomas S. Knight

Adelphi University

Thomas Hill Green

Thomas Hill Green

Thomas Hill Green
Philosopher of Rights

ANN R. CACOULLOS

Professor of Philosophy
Deree College, Athens

Twayne Publishers, Inc. :: New York

Library of Congress Cataloging in Publication Data

Cacoullos, Ann R

Thomas Hill Green: philosopher of rights.

(Twayne's World leader series)
Bibliography: p. 184.
1. Green, Thomas Hill, 1836-1882.
B1636.C3   192 [B]   73-21997
ISBN 0-8057-3683-2

MANUFACTURED IN THE UNITED STATES OF AMERICA

Dedicated to

My Mother and The Memory of My Father

Contents

About the Author

Ann Cacoullos was born in New York City and educated at Barnard College and Columbia University where she received the Ph.D. in philosophy. She has taught at the University of Minnesota and the Herbert H. Lehman College in the City University of New York. She is Assistant Professor of Philosophy at Deree College, Athens, Greece where she is residing at present with her husband and three children. Dr. Cacoullos is also on the teaching staff of the University of Maryland, European Division.

Preface and Acknowledgments

My aim in this book has been to focus on some ideas in Green's moral and political philosophy. A certain conception of rights, and the notions of self-realization and the common good, occupy a central place in Green's work. I have tried to reconstruct his theory of rights and to think further upon some of the foundations he laid.

The *Works of Thomas Hill Green* edited by R. L. Nettleship are in three volumes and were published from 1885 to 1888. These include all his philosophical writings except the *Prolegomena to Ethics*, which was published separately in 1883, edited by A. C. Bradley. Several editions of the *Lectures on the Principles of Political Obligation* have been published, the most recent in this country as an Ann Arbor Paperback by the University of Michigan Press, 1967. This contains the original preface by Bernard Bosanquet and the introduction by Lord Lindsay. The *Prolegomena* is now in a paperpack edition with an introduction by Ramon M. Lemos (New York: T. Y. Crowell, 1969).

Where I refer to an essay in the *Works* the abbreviation W. is used and the volume and page numbers given, e.g., W.I.9. References to Nettleship's *Memoir* on the life of T. H. Green in volume three of the *Works* are abbreviated to M. with the original roman numerals indicating the page; thus, M.xx. I have used the recent paperback editions of the *Prolegomena* and the *Lectures.* References to and quotations from these works are indicated by PE for the *Prolegomena* and LP for the *Lectures,* with the relevant section numbers, which are uniform in all editions; thus, 215PE, 19LP.

Nettleship's *Memoir* is the only full-length account of Green's life written by a contemporary who knew Green well. I have used this especially for the biographical chapter in this book and I wish to acknowledge my debt here. I would like also to record my debt to an excellent scholarly account of Green's milieu and of the various influences, especially religious and political, on his work. This is Melvin Richter's *The Politics of Conscience: T. H. Green and His Age* (Boston: Harvard, University Press, 1964). Though I have concentrated on different issues in this book, I want to thank Professor Richter for his encouragement.

My special thanks to Martin Golding, who set me onto Green when I was a graduate student at Columbia. I have learned a great deal from Golding's work on rights-theory. Thanks also to Bertram Bandman for encouraging me to publish my work on Green.

Chronology

1836   Born April 7 in Birkin, Yorkshire, the youngest of four children of Valentine Green, Rector of Birkin.

1837   Mother died. Educated by father until entrance to Rugby.

1850-   Schoolboy at Rugby.
1855

1855   Entered Balliol College, Oxford. Studied law and modern history.

1860   Elected fellow of Balliol. Lectured in ancient and modern history.

1862   Won Chancellor's prize for an essay upon novels. Undecided about future studies; took private pupils in philosophy.

1863   Signed the Thirty-nine Articles upon taking his M.A. degree. A pacifist, yet favored Northern cause in Civil War between the states.

1864   Unsuccessful candidate for the chair of moral philosophy at St. Andrews. Accepted an appointment as assistant commissioner of the royal commission upon middle-class schools. James Bryce and Matthew Arnold were fellow commissioners.

1866   Appointed senior dean at Balliol.

1867   Failed to secure Waynflete professorship of moral and metaphysical philosophy.

1870   As tutor, assisted headmaster in management of Balliol. Became leading exponent at the College of theories of Kant and Hegel. Delivered lay sermon "Witness to God," revealing unorthodox religious views.

1871	Married Charlotte Symonds on July 1.
1872	Reelected to fellowship at Balliol. Became active in local politics and educational problems. Supported the Liberal party.
1878	Elected to the Whyte professorship of moral philosophy. Delivered lectures that became basis of later publications. Symptoms of congenital heart disease.
1882	Died of blood poisoning on March 15.
1883	Publication of unfinished *Prolegomena to Ethics* under editorship of A. C. Bradley.
1885-1888	Works edited by R. L. Nettleship and collected for publication in three volumes.

CHAPTER 1

Introduction

When Thomas Hill Green became Whyte's Professor of Moral Philosophy at Oxford in 1878 he had already established a reputation as the university's leading philosopher and the town's most active citizen. These are the characteristic facts in the life of a man who, in the words of James Bryce, was "a singular instance of a metaphysician with a bent towards politics and practical life."[1] Unlike some great metaphysical system builders whom he admired, Green did not build a castle only to live in the shack next to it. He extended the forum for his ideas beyond the classroom to include the community of which he was a member. He believed that philosophical speculation when divorced from the moral life and moral action could become a "ridiculous conceit." (W.III.90)

In the years between 1880 and 1914 the major philosophical influence on both British thought and public policy was the school known as British Idealism launched by T. H. Green. This influence is little felt today; the reasons for the decline of the Idealists are familiar enough to students of philosophy. What is not often realized, however, is that the critical refutation of Idealist metaphysics which was undertaken in the first quarter of the twentieth century undermined some valuable themes in moral and political philosophy as well. It is in this area that the work of Green is most stimulating, and a study of some of his ideas can enrich the subject matter of ethics and political theory.

Green is said to have coined the phrase "political obligation." His ideas on the origins of, and grounds for, obedience to the state, however, are strongly reminiscent of those developed by Aristotle in *The Politics*. They are not original. His most distinctive contribution to political theory lies in what he had to say about rights. Green's theory of rights diverges from the strict Hegelian line taken by Idealists like Bradley and

13

Bernard Bosanquet. In effect his theory is neither "Idealist" nor "organic," for the basic elements in the theory derive not from Hegel but from Aristotle and Kant.

Green's theory of rights represents an attempt to break away from the classical natural rights doctrine without giving up the idea of "natural," or fundamental, human rights. Before Green, Jeremy Bentham and the English jurist John Austin had rejected the idea of natural law and natural rights. On their positivist account, rights properly speaking were constructs of the law. For these thinkers the only rights that exist are legal rights. Green argues that there are rights whose existence does not depend upon their recognition and enforcement by the law. These are "natural" rights, not in the sense that men are born with them, but in the sense that they are fundamental and valuable; they exist apart from the state and are secured by the mutual recognition by men of each other's claims. As against Locke, Green maintains that no right is innate. Rights are *made* by men. This fact does not diminish their significance. If anything, the existence of rights in any community becomes a measure of the moral and social achievement within that community. For Green, the existence of rights represents the degree to which individuals constitute a viable society. In this view, the conception of a right is far more significant than the one implicit in the classical natural rights doctrine. We should regard Green's theory as the first serious alternative we have to the doctrine of Locke and the natural law theorists.

All too frequently the idea of natural rights in political theory becomes a polemical tool in defense either of an unfettered individualism or, paradoxically, of leviathan states. This occurs whenever a theorist succumbs to what may be called the "chicken-egg sequence," when he attempts to formulate and elucidate the relations between individuals and society. The question is posed: which comes first—i.e., which is axiologically prior—the individual or society? This question is misleading if not unnatural: where, after all, are the Robinson Crusoes? Is not Man Friday always around, somewhere? Is it fruitful to try to decide who is more important, man-alone or man-in-society? Whether we like it or not, the basic unit for the theorist is man-in-society. The problem, as Green correctly realized, is to try to determine the extent to which the community can promote the freedom and self-development of each individual who is a member. This, among other things, is the social ideal, and rights are basic constituents of this ideal.

Green's work is difficult to read. Even though one of his favorite words when referring to language was "swing," his prose emphatically does not swing. It is ponderous, repetitive, and often obscure. In a period when there is a high premium on clarity, at least this fact about Green's style is surely enough to limit his readership. But there is another and more important factor which separates Green's order and style of thinking from the contemporary variety. His approach to the subject matter of moral and political philosophy is neither analytical nor sociological. It is, in a special sense of the term, ideological.

Categories of this sort are meant to provide very general descriptions of philosophical inclination rather than method. In Green we have several different sorts of philosophical "bent," not the least of which is his metaphysical one. Like Plato, Hobbes, and Hegel, Green tried to provide a metaphysical framework for his moral and political concepts. Indeed, he has been criticized for attempting to deduce or derive the facts of moral and political experience from some ultimate metaphysical principles. But Green's political and social doctrines manifest as well a peculiarly moral deliberation on the good life, on ends and ideals which can provide a basis for political practices and institutions. Insofar as he was intent on elucidating the moral basis of the state and rights held by individuals, his approach may be said to be ideological. This may be defined as "the form of political thinking in which the *emphasis* falls neither on philosophical analysis and deduction, nor on sociological generalization, but on moral reflection—on elaborating and advocating conceptions of the good life and of describing the forms of social action and organization necessary for their achievement."[2]

It is not that Green advocates a particular political system; neither does he present a list of fundamental, inalienable rights. An ideological approach is not to be confused with "ideology" or "ideological politics." It is the sort of questions Green raised and the issues he concentrated on that reveal his ideological approach. At the outset of the *Lectures on the Principles of Political Obligation* he writes: "My purpose is to consider the moral function or object served by law, or by the system of rights and obligations which the state enforces, and in so doing to discover the true ground or justification for obedience to law." (1LP) The interest expressed in these words is a moral interest, and Green's political philosophy is to a large extent an extension and application of his moral doctrine. His theory of rights is based upon his conception of the moral end or the good life for man.

Green's analysis of rights and his theory of political obligation are both instances of the moral urge expressing itself in political and social philosophy. Some persons are put off by this urge or eagerness to consider in moral terms issues which are clearly political and social and which require less fancy and more attention to the facts of actual social and political life. It is not clear to many, for instance, that man has a *moral end* as Green supposed, nor is it obvious that there can exist in society anything like a common denominator of sentiment and idea which acts like a creative force in the shaping of political institutions and the allocation of rights. In arguing that there is an end for man and that society and the state are both products of man's fundamental interest in morality and the good life, Green appears, so it is argued, to overlook the intricate psychological and sociological forces that come into play in the relations between individuals. His thesis on the common good appears to commit him to a simplistic if not unrealistic explanation of man's readiness to acknowledge the claims of others. Moreover, to say as he does that rights are determined by reference to, and on the grounds of, a common good is not to say what these rights are—what, that is, one ought to be entitled to, and how conflicts between various claims are to be resolved. And these would seem to be the important, pragmatic issues.

It is argued today that the categories and assumptions of old-fashioned philosophers like Green seem muddled and that we are fortunate to be rid of such notions as "the common good." Appeals to the common good are more often than not appeals to a chimera, and *moral* reflection on the nature of man or the good life does little to advance our understanding of the notion of a right. Such reflection seems to produce tautologies at most.

The foregoing might be considerations which argue against Green's approach to the issues of rights-theory. To the extent that they do prevail, and there is evidence in the literature that weight is attached to such considerations, there would seem to be little to be gained from reading Green except as a historical curiosity.[3] But we need not accept this judgment, for there is value in Green's approach as well as in the answers he gave to the various questions he posed. The moral framework in which he placed his theory of rights alerted him to a host of issues and factors which his predecessors had ignored. As Melvin Richter notes, "Aware of the socially shared values that underlie law and political machinery, Green thought it important to understand how the individual is affected by membership in groups, a relationship which ought to be, but seldom is, considered by theorists of rights and duties. Thus the problems he posed were significant as were the answers he suggested."[4]

Green's ideological approach in the theory of rights is exemplified in the main question he posed and tried to answer, namely, "why rights at all?" This is not the only question one can ask about rights, but it is certainly one of the important ones; for it is not intuitively clear without further argument that certain claims ought to be acknowledged and respected as a matter of right. Green's theory takes its start from his criticism of the view that certain rights require no justification. The question "why rights at all?" might sound peculiar to a John Locke. One does not, after all, give reasons for *natural* rights; one does not have to justify what is given, indeed, God-given. But, as we've noted, rights for Green are not given; they do not exist automatically when a man is born. They are made by men for reasons which have to do with their conscious needs, ideals, and purposes.

According to Green we cannot understand the nature of rights and what it means to have a right unless we inquire into the reasons or grounds for rights on the one hand, and how rights come to exist on the other. We have to ask, "How it is that certain powers are recognized by men in their intercourse with each other as powers that should be exercised, or of which the possible exercise should be secured." (24LP)

The important ideas in the theory of rights are the personal ideal of self-realization, the notions of community, equality, and recognition, and the social ideal of the common good. Green's explicit thesis is that the individual cannot have rights apart from his membership in a community and apart from a relation of *isotes,* or equality, which exists between him and others. Rights require the community as well as an ideal of the good life which informs the actions of members of the community. Moreover, rights are made by recognition. Critics have seized upon this idea and accused Green of making legality a necessary condition for all rights. But the force of the idea lies elsewhere. Green's insistence on recognition is, among other things, an insistence on a vigilant, conscientious citizenry as a condition for the existence of rights. Rights, unlike trees, are not "out there" to be touched and used at will. Whether we view them as demands, needs, claims, expectations, or entitlements, one thing is certain: they are fragile and they require, like the individuals who aspire to them, the proper environment in which to flourish. For Green, the proper setting is a community in which every member recognizes a common good as his own. Adherence to such an ideal promotes the readiness of each member to acknowledge the claims of others.

We may argue that Green's requirement is too strong and even unrealistic. But his attention to what I have called the proper environment surely focuses on an important condition for the existence of rights and indeed of the good life: a person's realization and willingness to grant that his own successful claiming and achievement of a right is contingent upon the successful claiming by other persons similarly situated.

A great part of the *Lectures* and the *Prolegomena to Ethics* is given to Green's criticism of the views of Hobbes, Locke, Spinoza, Rousseau, Austin, Bentham, and Mill. It would seem as though Green stood wholly apart from the work of these men. Yet he worked within an English tradition as well as without. While his epistemology is in the main Kantian and his moral theory incorporates Aristotelian as well as Kantian elements, his political and social doctrines embrace some important ideas of the British Utilitarians. For instance, Green adheres to the idea that power is integral to rights, an idea common to both Hobbes and Austin, though in opposition to the latter he does not equate "power" and "right." Again, he adopts Austin's view that sovereignty lies with a determinate person or persons, but agrees with Rousseau and Kant against Austin that obedience to the sovereign is a function not of the sovereign's command but of the subject's will. With Bentham, Green maintains that each person is to count for one and no one for more than one, but he fills out this formula with the Kantian idea of the equal moral worth of each individual. The convergence of several issues between Locke and Green has been noted by writers. Locke's doctrine of the individual's natural political virtue arising out of "a symmetry in reason between all of us" lends itself readily to Green's thesis that communal living and the existence of rights are products of the "rational recognition by certain human beings of a common well-being which is their well-being." (117LP) Yet Green remained at odds with Locke's theory of natural rights. Finally, there is Mill. It would seem that Green and Mill are poles apart, for the latter is the great defender of what has been called the negative conception of freedom while Green, following Rousseau, is an exponent of positive freedom. But Green is within the tradition of Mill when he argues that governments must remove obstacles to the free development of citizens, and Mill the reformer would concur with Green that the state must provide opportunities for individual self-realization.

Green's name has been linked to the theory of the "new liberalism" which emerged in the latter part of the nineteenth century. It is true that Green was an important spokesman for the new liberalism, but it is also true that he was a child of the old, classical liberalism. As noted above, on some issues he remained within a definite tradition begun by Hobbes and Locke.

Scholars have wondered how new Green's variety of liberalism in fact was. We may ask whether Green was prepared to defend a program of radical social change in order to ensure to each individual a morally significant place within the community. A sense of the importance of *koinonia,* or community, dominates Green's social and political theory, and we must view his vaguely defined notion of self-realization in the light of Aristotle's recommendation that self-fulfillment and *eudaimonia,* or the good life, are achieved in part by the individual's participation in communal affairs. But Green does not outline a definite program of social change. Later writers who were influenced by him and who adopted his theory of the common good were to argue for the sort of social and political reform which in the early part of the twentieth century was considered far to the left of a moderate liberalism. In Green's case we can only interpolate. I would suggest that since the dominant talk in his political theory is about rights, whether of the individual or of society, his ideal of self-realization and the common good may be an ideal of social justice. It may be that, for Green, the ultimate moral worth of every individual is to be secured as a matter of justice and not of charity or other prudential considerations. If this is so, then, as one writer put it, Green's ideal "can provide the ethical ground for a program of social change far more radical" than liberalism has ordinarily defended.[5]

CHAPTER 2

Life and Vocation

Green and Philosophy

When Thomas Hill Green entered Oxford's Balliol College as an undergraduate in 1855, the study of philosophy was not what it is today. Like many others of his age and background, Green enrolled in the school of *Literae Humaniores,* or "Greats," where the chief emphasis was on a reading of certain Latin and Greek texts. The great works of antiquity dominated the curriculum not only in text but in spirit. Aristotle was read as a revered authority. In his lectures on the ideals of a university Cardinal Newman pronounced that "to think correctly is to think like Aristotle and we are his disciples whether we will or no."[1] But this is not all. Philosophical works seemed to serve the purposes of rhetoric, whether political or religious. J. A. Symonds, a contemporary of Green, wrote, "At Oxford . . . philosophy was studied mainly from the rhetorical point of view. We were taught to write upon a vast variety of debatable topics and to acquire some smatterings of what the several schools had uttered on them; but there was no robust mental training, no process by which man was compelled to think. Worse than that, aspirants after honours were habituated to deal cleverly with words and phrases, and to criticise without substantial knowledge. . . ."[2]

In the last four decades of the nineteenth century many notable persons were to rebel against the curriculum and the methods of teaching which surrounded the study of philosophy. Green's role in transforming the study of philosophy at Oxford was decisive. In one sense the groundwork for the "revolution in philosophy" which occurred in the first decades of the twentieth century was begun by Green several years before. It may seem odd to attribute to a British Idealist a role in a movement which was in part a reaction to

Idealist metaphysics. But Green's contribution was not to an original philosophical system. It was rather his defense of philosophy as an autonomous, professional discipline that marked the beginnings of the course philosophy was to follow at Oxford. As the historian R. C. K. Ensor points out, it was in effect the Idealists who professionalized philosophy.[3]

What was Green's attitude on the matter? First of all, he believed that the philosophical study of great texts constituted a discipline quite distinct from a historical or literary reading. The former presupposed critical attention to what was being said and whether this was meaningful and correct. As such, a philosophical approach might initially be destructive and only incidentally appreciative, according to Green. Further, one who concentrated heavily on the history of philosophy might in fact have very little interest in philosophical issues themselves. "It is possible," Green wrote, "for knowledge about philosophies to flourish inversely as the knowledge of philosophy. The revived interest which is noticeable in the history of philosophy may be an indication either of philosophical rigour or of philosophical decay." (W.1.4) An interest in the literary history of philosophy is often the result of a skeptical attitude about the possibility of achieving truth by means of philosophical thinking. Such skepticism renders philosophy "a matter about which there has been much guessing by great intellectuals, but no definite truth is to be attained." (W.1.4)

Green reacted as much to this attitude as to the opposite, which viewed every philosophical work as authoritative. Neither skepticism nor unexamined appreciation served the cause of philosophy. For Green, we miss the whole point of philosophical endeavor unless we approach each philosopher with two questions in mind: "What was his problem and what was his method?" (W.I.5) In the process of dealing with a work, of trying to estimate its significance, the critic may have to be destructive:

It will seem as if, while we talk of their value, we were impertinently trying to "pull them to pieces." But those who understand the difference between philosophical failures, which are so because they are anachronisms, and those which in their failure have brought out a new truth and compelled a step forward in the progress of thought, will understand that a process, which looks like pulling a great philosopher to pieces, may be the true way of showing reverence for his greatness. It is a Pharisaical way of building the sepulchres of philosophers to profess their doctrine or extol their genius without making their spirit our own. [W.I.5]

These words taken from the "Introductions" Green wrote for an edition of Hume's work express very clearly his belief that philosophy, its study and its practice, is primarily critical, and its aim the advancement of knowledge. It was neither a training ground for orators nor a literary device for the achievement of educated guesses. The study and the writing of philosophy required special training which until Green's time Oxford failed to provide.

For both their approach and their commitment to philosophy as an autonomous discipline, Green and some of his illustrious students, notably F. H. Bradley, were to be considered odd men out in the Oxford of the 1860s and 1870s, especially by the Master of Balliol, Benjamin Jowett. Many readers today know Jowett as the great translator of Plato. In fact, he was a powerful force in the reform of undergraduate education at Oxford University. His quarrel with Green, a former pupil, revolved around many issues which we need not consider here. But two of these must be mentioned. The first has to do with Jowett's mistrust of Idealist metaphysics, of which Green and Bradley were exponents; the second with the teaching of philosophy.

For many years after he was elected Fellow of Balliol College Green had to teach the prescribed courses in the Greats curriculum which included, in addition to the works of Aristotle, the history of early Greek thought, Plato, and the New Testament. These were not the subjects Green himself would have chosen to teach had he been able to choose. As Nettleship tells us in his *Memoir*, Green was neither by inclination nor by temperament a classics scholar. Furthermore, he did not see his task as essentially one of preparing undergraduates to answer questions likely to appear on examinations. To fill what he took to be a real need in the college, he initiated some advanced classes in philosophy for a select group of students who were later to become prominent scholars and philosophers in their own right. This effort evoked Jowett's rebuke, and Green was for a time prevented from teaching altogether in the college. He wrote in a letter to A. C. Bradley that he "was not prepared for the permanence of his [Jowett's] desire entirely to expel philosophy from Balliol."[4] As a matter of fact, Jowett did not want to rid Balliol of philosophy, for he considered himself both a historian and a critic of philosophy. But he did oppose certain philosophical trends which through Green were infiltrating the college. He believed that metaphysics exercised "a fatal influence over the mind in destroying the power of observation and of acquiring knowledge."[5] As far as Jowett could see, Green's lectures promoted the sort of jargon that was likely to be more confusing than enlightening. More importantly, he seemed to believe further that, though reading Plato and Aristotle was important, philosophy itself did not require any specialized training. Its purpose was simply to instill certain intellectual qualities which would be useful to the bright young men of Oxford in their pursuit of political careers. For Jowett, philosophy was supposed to sharpen one's wits. In Green he found a man who thought that metaphysics was a source of knowledge and truth and that philosophy itself was a professional discipline.

It is possible that Jowett did not clearly distinguish between two separate issues, namely, Green's own style of philosophizing, and the latter's view, independent of his metaphysics, that philosophy had, in the words of Bradley, "a business of its own."[6] Many contemporary philosophers would be in complete sympathy with some of Jowett's judgments. But even those who would subscribe to his condemnation of Idealist metaphysics will insist that philosophy does indeed have a business of its own even if its main concerns are no longer those Green envisioned.

As a tutor and later when he lectured on the subjects of his choice, Green did more than anyone else at the time to rescue philosophy from its continued absorption by classical scholarship and theology. In his hands it became a strict discipline requiring careful, often arduous study and justifying further, postgraduate study and teaching. Green did not introduce a new method of doing philosophy nor did he put to sophisticated uses the new symbolic logic that was emerging in the nineteenth century. It was rather a new attitude that Green fostered and best expressed in his own abiding commitment to philosophy. Nettleship writes, "Philosophy was to him the medium in which the theoretic impulse, the impulse to see and feel things more clearly and intensely than everyday life allows, found its most congenial satisfaction." (M.lxvi) He was as serious about philosophy as most persons today are about science; and it is this seriousness which he injected into the curriculum, not, however, to proselytize or to propagandize. Green deliberately eschewed the role of seer or lawgiver. He did not care to attract disciples and, curiously, was "painfully conscious how little direct result can be expected from the study or teaching of philosophy." (M.lxvi-vii) But whoever felt an enthusiasm for the subject matter found in Green a careful and impartial critic. Far from turning undergraduates into either prigs or theologians, Green inspired the need for critical analysis. He is reported to have remarked that the philosopher cannot deal in mysteries, that it is his "prime business to take account of what and how we think."[7] This is sober talk for one who was and has been charged with being muddle-headed.

I do not want to suggest that before Green, English thinkers like Hobbes, Hume, and Mill were not serious when they wrote. They were, but their efforts were exerted outside the university. Green *taught* philosophy and encountered it, therefore, in this light—namely, as a subject worthy of professional attention with a curriculum all its own. On the other hand, he was more sensitive than most in recognizing that if the study and practice of philosophy are divorced from practical life they become mere conceits.

Early Life and Student Days

Green's life, as his principal biographer tells us, was spent in "thinking, speaking, and writing about philosophy and religion, and in quietly promoting the political and social interests" of the town of Oxford, where he lived as a student and later as a married man. (M.xi) Nettleship goes on to observe that these facts scarcely make for "striking biography." There are no amusing stories one can tell to spike the narrative. There were no cataclysmic events in Green's life, and Nettleship's *Memoir* is a narrative of unrelieved seriousness and esteem.

But this accurately reflects the sort of life Green lived.

He was born on April 7, 1836, in the Yorkshire village of Berkin, the youngest of four children, two sons and two daughters. Like many upper-middle-class boys growing up in nineteenth-century England, Green received his early education at home. He was tutored by his father, the Reverend Valentine Green, until he was fourteen years of age and, in 1850, went to Rugby, a public school which had acquired some fame under the headmastership of Dr. Arnold, the father of the poet and critic Matthew Arnold. A portrait of the young Green at Rugby composed from reports of teachers and reminiscences of friends reveals a student not nearly as studious as his classmates. He is described as "indolent" and "puzzled," possessing at the same time a "certain grave rebelliousness." He was invariably late with his papers and exercises and did not seem interested in learning. When he finally won a prize at Rugby it was for his translation of a passage from John Milton's *Areopagitica*. The text apparently was exciting enough to arouse his attention. It was no coincidence that this was an essentially political text and for its time a rebellious one.

Green had trouble adjusting not only to academic requirements but also to school authorities. On the first matter he wrote to his father, "I always find that if I cram myself with the ideas of others, my own will vanish." (M.xiii) This mental independence cost him the loss of several awards. On the second issue, that is, his relation to school authorities, he was a rebel of sorts insofar as he went his own way when he believed the rules were not right. There was always in Green a struggle between his conscience and his sense of duty, though the latter helped him to overcome his personal aversion to the authorities; he acceded to them whenever he felt they served a noble purpose. Thus, he defended the monetorial system at Rugby because he believed it was the only way to stop the bullying of weak and friendless students.

Naturally shy and withdrawn, he impressed everyone as a serious fellow. Both at Rugby and later on at Oxford, Green avoided parties. On Sunday afternoon he walked by himself in the fields because, he would say, it was only there he could worship God best. There is little evidence of an early interest in philosophy, though one account by Green's schoolmate at

Rugby and future philosophical adversary Henry Sidgwick reveals something of a budding metaphysical bent in Green. Sidgwick recalls that when they were out together walking one day they came upon a bridge and Green "endeavoured to make me understand that we each of us saw a different bridge." (M.xv)

The days he spent at Oxford as a student were relatively uneventful, though it is important to record various opinions he expressed at this time, for these provide a useful background to the issues that came to dominate his thinking as a philosopher and as a citizen. His first impressions of Oxford, recorded in a letter to his father, were mainly negative:

The insides of the Colleges are strangely incongruous with the outside. The finest colleges are the most corrupt, the functionaries from the heads to the servants being wholly given to quiet dishonesty, and the undergraduates to sensual idleness. . . . I shall be happy there if I can work hard, but the temptations to idleness seem inumerable. My chief ones would be those most luxurious canoes in which one can paddle for hours under the most delicious shade. . . . [M.xvi]

As it turned out Green did not succumb to either the delicious shade or the general revelry of Oxford undergraduate life. This was not solely because he was "mature," "never silly," "never flippant," and lacked a sense of romance, but also because he did not seem able to make his peace with what he called the "obnoxious breed" of Oxford undergraduates. Very early in his life Green aligned himself with the less privileged segments of English society. A fellow student at Oxford describes him as having a great "love for social equality" and a powerful "sense of the dignity of simple human nature." He had a strong belief "in the duty of approaching the people directly and getting them to form and express their own ideas." (M.xix) A. V. Dicey, who knew Green at Oxford, commented in a letter to Green's wife that while most young men at the university dabbled in "romantic politics," Green was anxious to impress on everyone the evils of pauperism and the need for reform.[8]

The political leadership of mid-Victorian England, dominated by the jingoist programs of Lord Palmerston, depressed Green. It was the speeches and reform efforts of John Bright that attracted him as a student. When he defended Bright in a speech to the Oxford Union in 1858 Green found, however, that he was in a minority of two. The cause of the workers which Bright championed did not elicit the sympathies of Oxford undergraduates at this time, and Green's adherence to Bright and Richard Cobden earned for him the label "radical." He was considered "an extreme man, an ultra-radical in politics, an ultra-liberal in religious opinion." (M.xlv) This judgment probably reveals more about the general climate of opinion in mid-nineteenth-century Oxford than it does about Green's views. As a matter of fact, he was always extremely reserved when expressing his political views, both as a student and later as a tutor. It is very difficult to determine the extent to which Green was a radical, especially since the term has covered a wide range of views both philosophical and political. Some of the papers Green read to the Old Mortality, an undergraduate society to which the better students belonged, might very well have been considered radical by his audience. But the term itself implies either too much or too little and it might be well to avoid it as a summary description of Green's views. We are on safer ground if we go beyond the labels to the views themselves.

None of the papers Green wrote for the Old Mortality are preserved, but we have some idea of the content of two of these from the minutes that were kept and from the journal of A. V. Dicey, Green's classmate. In a paper he read entitled "National Life," Green expressed contempt for "national honour" and "imperial greatness." The one sentence which impressed Dicey was: "Let the flag of England be dragged through the dirt rather than sixpence be added to the taxes which weigh on the poor." (M.xxi) The words are strong and probably shocked even those who were mildly nationalistic. The fact is that Green never succumbed to the fever of nationalism that raged in the nineteenth century. While he was as enthusiastic as his fellow undergraduates about the movements for national freedom abroad—he defended Mazzini in a speech before the Oxford Union—he was far more preoccupied with the plight of the working class and the poor in England. If he had little respect for national honor and greatness, this was because these had come to mean imperial expansion abroad. As such, the nation to which allegiance was called for represented the political vanity of a few rather than the social aspirations of the many. Green reacted to the marriage of the Prince of Wales with the melancholy thought of "how much these festivities do to degrade the people. I take it this one royal wedding postpones the chance of real reform a decade or more." (M.xliv)

In his own mind the national priorities were clear. Government had to concern itself with the problems of social justice; this is what national life was really about. Of the essays Green wrote as an undergraduate—he never handed these in on time, either—many still exist and one in particular, entitled "Loyalty," contains in embryonic form the ideas he developed in the *Lectures on the Principles of Political Obligation.* The characteristic Green style is already evident in this essay. One passage is especially interesting:

The truly loyal man is not he who shouts for king and constitution, or who yields a blind obedience to the routine of existing institutions, but he who looks beyond these to the universal laws of the common reason of man and in reverence for this yields a willing and hearty obedience to the rules in which it embodies itself for the establishment of right dealing in society; rules which, except so far as they have been distorted by violence, have only varied to adapt themselves to the varying affairs of men. And if loyalty is the national enemy of tyranny . . . so is it no less opposed to a selfish seeking for individual gain. Recognizing the duty owed by all to the supreme power and common good of the state, the loyal man is bound to his fellow-citizens in the unity of a common object, which gives to the private pursuits of his daily life their value and spiritual meaning. [M.xxiii]

The contemporary reader of such an essay, and indeed of much of Green's mature work, may find himself now nodding in agreement, now vigorously shaking his head, and sometimes trying to do both at the same time. But then, Green was never known either for the clarity of his writing or the fluent delivery of his lectures. One story has it that very many times at the end of a lecture which was not "easy to follow" Green "had become so contorted that he had to be untied by friendly hands."[9]

Still, the passage quoted above is fairly clear in its meaning. Its theme is the conditions presupposed by a healthy political society. In the chapters following we shall be exploring the theme at length. For now, I think it is important to note that very early in his career Green committed himself to the view that political obligation or the duty to obey the law required neither the suspension of reason nor the forfeiture of individual autonomy. To the extent that the laws of a state did require this, they were distorted. Green does refer to the "supreme power" of the state, but it is well to bear in mind that for him the machinery of government as well as the private rights of individuals are all constituents of a common good. Basic to Green's theme is the belief—which pervades his ethics and political philosophy—that moral and legal rules are the product of one source, man's rational decision making. Rules vary from society to society, but they all possess a common core which Green called the "divine principle" or the "common reason" in man. A difficult position to argue for, but that Green wanted to defend such a view is clear from what he wrote.

As far as Green was concerned the England of his day was corrupt, having reneged on all important issues. On Palmerston's death in 1865 Green wrote to his father, "I cannot pretend to be sorry, being persuaded that he did about as much harm as it is possible for an individual Englishman to do nowadays." (M.xxiii) The age of Palmerston had opted for a certain type of prereform, laissez-faire liberalism which served best the needs of the commercial and industrial middle class. The ends sought were the self-seeking aims of privileged individuals. Social and political inequalities were bolstered by moral lassitude. That there was great sympathy in England for the South during the American Civil War convinced Green of the country's shallowness. While he himself had powerful antiwar feelings—he opposed the Crimean War, for instance—he did not hesitate to take sides when a great issue was at stake. Advocates for the Southern cause accused the North of aggression and held its republican institutions responsible for the war. Green defended the North in a speech to the Oxford Union in 1863: "It is not a republic that is answerable for this war, but a slave-holding, slave-breeding and slave-burning oligarchy, on whom the curse of God and humanity rests." (M.xliii) Green was a pacificist. He was to argue against war, even the idea of a justified war, in the *Lectures*. But during the Civil War he cheered every Northern victory. If there is a trace of contradiction here, it is well to remember that Green also believed that a nation had a moral responsibility to all its people and not merely to the vocal privileged few. It is perhaps to his credit that he did not always try to reconcile his opposing views.

Life as Fellow and Tutor

The life Green led as a student and later as a tutor was quiet. Despite his strong feelings on certain matters he was no agitator, and his poor health as well as his inability to speak well on a platform discouraged him from embarking on a political career. Nor did he see himself cut out for the ministry, despite his profound religious faith. He was one of Jowett's best students and in the summer of 1859 gained a first class in the school. He was employed in 1860 to lecture on ancient and modern history, and toward the end of that year was elected a Fellow of Balliol College. Even though he was an unsuccessful candidate for a chair of moral philosophy at St. Andrews, he had decided that his vocation lay in teaching. In 1866 he was appointed senior dean at Balliol. His duties were to read weekly essays, manage the college examinations, and overlook the hall and kitchen. By 1867 he settled down to the work of a college tutor. He was probably the first layman to hold that office. As a tutor Green impressed pupils and other Fellows with his seriousness and his commitment to the work he was doing. He always seemed "to be working things out" when he lectured and so his lectures were always in the making. (M.lxviii) Nettleship tells us that "his chief strength lay in a comparatively new and narrow branch of study, unconnected with much of the ordinary curriculum of the university." (M.lxi) This "new and narrow branch" was philosophy. In 1878 Green was appointed Whyte's Professor of Moral Philosophy.

The enthusiasm he kindled in his students was not for any particular doctrine but for philosophy, period. If asked to say what they believed in "they could only have answered 'in philosophy.'" (M.lxviii) The group around Green was described or perhaps ridiculed as "a society for looking at things as a whole." It would be unfair to conclude from this that Green was starting a vogue that would quickly pass. While his own metaphysics did pass, philosophy itself did not. But there was, as his biographer indicates, a tendency to view with suspicion the vagueness that surrounded the subject matter. In this regard, Nettleship's own remarks are profound and worth quoting in full:

Philosophy, indeed, like other great subjects cannot be taught without exposing itself to travesty; it becomes sentimental in the weak enthusiast, mechanical in the able philistine. And each form of the philosophical spirit has the special defects of its own qualities: one lends itself to a superior cynicism, another to complacent omniscience, a third to unctuous rhetoric. No system of teaching or examination can avoid these incidental evils; the only defense against them lies in the constant apprehension of them; but whenever the subject is taught by a person of more than ordinary force, they will inevitably appear in one form or another, exciting the ridicule of enemies and the alarm of friends. [M.lxviii]

Perhaps the words we choose today to describe the incidental evils to which Nettleship alludes would differ somewhat. Few claim omniscience but many evidence cynicism. Able practitioners of philosophy on both sides of the Atlantic continue to be sensitive to the threat and charge of travesty. Doing philosophy involves one unavoidably in *hubris,* yet the speculative impulse is profoundly human. Neither sentimentality nor mechanical sophistication is satisfactory. The philosopher indeed has to be more critical than most of the methods he employs both in raising questions and answering them. More often than not he has to be content with projecting a problem clearly rather than posing an answer.

Green did not bypass the problems he confronted, but perhaps he rushed too quickly into solutions. It is true he was deeply aware of the inadequacy and confusion in his own theories and he might have removed these had he lived to edit his own work. We can only assume now that he tried to guard against being either sentimental or mechanical.

The subjects he taught were determined in part by the requirements of the curriculum and in part by his own choice.

With the exception of Mill's *Logic,* modern philosophy was not yet a part of the curriculum. Philosophical courses centered around certain works of Aristotle and Plato. The *Nicomachean Ethics* of Aristotle was one of Green's principal subjects. It was Aristotle's view of the rational nature of man that attracted him and became a basic thesis in his own version of the principle of self-realization. According to Henry Sidgwick, Green did not interpret the Greeks correctly.[10] Green held that the ethics of Plato and Aristotle rest on a conception of a free or pure morality, on a disinterested interest in the good. This, according to Sidgwick, was a Kantian idea and quite alien to the Greeks. For the latter, moral action is not the less moral either for deriving from self-interest or for serving the interests of the self. Sidgwick's criticism of Green on this score is sound, but this is a large issue which we shall not examine here. We can note, however, that Green does have in common with the Greeks one basic concern which is best summed up in the phrase "character ethics." The fact of moral quandary did not capture Green's attention as much as the conditions for the development of moral character. Not what shall I do, what rules shall I follow, but who am I to become and how, is the question Green raises in his moral philosophy. And this is a very Greek sort of question. True, he did waver between a Kantian and an Aristotelian ethic, though perhaps "waver" is not the right word. He tried to combine the two.

Green's most important lectures, however, and his chief contribution to the philosophical curriculum, consisted of a critical exposition of English philosophy in the seventeenth and eighteenth centuries. It was Green who brought Hume to Oxford. The substance of these lectures form the content of the "Introductions," which was Green's contribution to a new edition of Hume's work published in 1874-75. There are over 380 pages of criticism. This edition by Green and E. Gosse is still highly regarded today. Green also lectured on Kant's *Critique of Pure Reason,* which was another innovation at Oxford.

By 1874 Green had formulated his own metaphysical principles. As Nettleship points out in his fine summary, these ideas are not new, they are "the common heritage . . . of all idealism." (M.Ixxx) I shall not deal with Green's metaphysics in this book. His distinctive contribution as a philosopher does not lie here but, if anywhere, in his moral and political ideas. It may be argued that we cannot separate his moral from his metaphysical principles. In Green's mind, certainly, they were inseparable. But his ethics of self-realization and his theory of rights and the common good do not stand or fall with the belief in a universe which is self-conscious, whose unity is sustained by a divine principle. That Green tried to ground his ethics in his metaphysics is true; that he did not have to do so is also true. If one wants to maintain that, in making a decision either to act in a certain way or to observe certain rules or to recognize another's claim, a man is employing his rational faculty rather than simply feeling certain emotions, and that this employment renders the decision peculiarly "moral," one does not have to appeal to a divine principle in man as the moralizing agent. Green could very well argue that reason is not always the slave of the passions without any metaphysical underpinning. The extent to which his metaphysics strengthens his case for the moral ideal is debatable. It has probably done the opposite, especially since the metaphysical jargon frequently conceals what might be a viable ethical theory.

Political Activity and Views

An examination of the views Green held on the subjects of political and social reform, education, and religion affords some insight into the sort of doctrines he tried to develop in his moral and political philosophy. In the remaining sections of this chapter we will consider these in turn.

In 1867 Green made his first appearance on a political platform when he spoke before the Oxford Reform League. The occasion was a meeting to consider the reform bill introduced by the conservative government in Parliament. This was the Great Reform Bill which extended the franchise. Opposition to the bill was expected from capitalists and members of the educated classes. Much of the best of Green, the politically involved citizen, emerges in the speech he made. He moved that the League support continued agitation for reform. He argued that the conflict in government was no longer between Lords and Commons but between the latter and the people.

The members of the lower house were largely great landowners. Capitalists and landowners bred and bribed each other and created an exclusive oligarchy which, according to Green, was simply "the highest outcome of a flunkeyism which pervades English society from the top to the bottom, and is incompatible with any healthy political life." (M.cxi) As he could not sympathize with a class that excluded others from participating in the political life, so too he rejected the claims of the educated. "As to the educated class," he said, "it is hard to know what that means. Everyone who wears a good coat, or reads the *Times* or the *Saturday Review,* believes himself to belong to the educated class." (M.cxi) Those fortunate enough to share in higher learning were using it as a device to insulate themselves from the rest of society. Green could not abide "the spirit of protection and exclusion," as he called it, that infected higher education. It was necessary therefore to oppose the capitalists and the educated class.

To the skeptical attitude of what could result from the enfranchisement of the people, Green replied in another speech that this was not the issue: "Untie the man's legs, and then it will be time to speculate how he will walk." (M.cxii) In this same speech delivered in February, 1868, he advocated reform of the land laws. The system of great estates, according to Green, encouraged vast economic inequalities, with great wealth at one end and abysmal poverty at the other. Agricultural workers lacked an interest in the soil because they had no security of tenure on the land. Individual benevolence or "ten-thousand soup kitchens" were inadequate to lift farmers out of their poverty. The solution lay in governmental legislation which would limit the power of the landlord to determine the future disposition of an estate. The existing system of land settlements and bequests had to be changed.

Green's views on the nature and extent of reform are summed up neatly in his lecture on "Liberal Legislation and Freedom of Contract." Green inherited the ideology of limited state action inherent in laissez-faire liberalism. The idea that the task of government is mainly negative and lies primarily in the removal of restraints on individual enterprise dominated the legislative programs of Peel and Cobden. Various acts liberating trade and industry were defended in the name of individual freedom. The aim of liberal legislation had been and continued to be the removal of "all obstructions which the law can remove to the free development of English citizens." (M.cxx) With this aim, Green was in complete sympathy. That is to say, he felt there was a basic uniformity of principle in the work of all political reform: "The nature of the general political reformer is perhaps always the same. The passion for improving mankind, in its ultimate object, does not vary," he wrote in "Liberal Legislation." (W.III.367) But the type of legislation required to bring about the ultimate end of improvement in the human situation differs from generation to generation. It may be that instead of simply removing restraints on individual action the state may have to interfere with certain hitherto free arrangements in order to promote the freedom of a greater number of persons. According to Green this was in effect the principle which inspired the reform legislation in the last decades of the nineteenth century. In the name of freedom, though freedom in a positive sense, government could no longer remain minimal. Its task was to secure equal freedom for all. But to do this it had to interfere with the freedom of some.

Green's concept of positive freedom, which is at the basis of his conception of the aims of public and political policy, is fundamentally an egalitarian concept. In the final analysis the programs of reform Green supported were those intended to secure goods and services to all men equally, for this would make the "life of citizenship" possible for all. It seems to me that this egalitarian dimension in Green's concept is not fully appreciated. According to some critics the idea of positive freedom is supposed to refer to the liberation of man's "truer, higher" self, and Green is taken to advocate a moral function for government. But Green is quite clear that as far as the moral improvement of the individual is concerned the task of government is mainly negative. The state does not exist to promote morality, for in the very nature of the case only the individual can do this. Moral improvement is a matter of inner private space. The state, however, can alter significantly the nature of the public spaces in which men move. Moreover, it can and ought to make certain matters more "public," that is, of general, communal concern. Contracts affecting labor and disposition of property, where these affect others besides the owners; health, liquor traffic (for us today it would be drug traffic), education, are all matters that must engage the attention of government, which is ideally the most public of all spaces. In these areas the state must interfere to restrict the activities of some persons for the sake of the freedom of all. Green declares: "Our modern legislation then with reference to labour, and education and health, involving as it does manifold interference with freedom of contract, is justified on the ground that it is the business of the state, not indeed directly to promote moral goodness, for that, from the very nature of moral goodness, it cannot do, but to maintain the conditions without which a free exercise of the human faculties is impossible." (W.III.374)

Historians consider Green an exponent of the New Liberalism which, in contrast to the old theory of the early and middle nineteenth century, moved closer to a concept of the welfare state. It is arguable, however, whether Green was willing to go as far as some socialists did go in the twentieth century. Melvin Richter remarks that "when Green spoke of 'positive freedom' he did not commit himself to any use of state power beyond that in fact advocated by Gladstone and Bright."[11] It is true that he was sensitive to the danger of overlegislation, but on this issue he was far more wary of centralized state power than of undue interference with individual action. Green did mistrust the bureaucratic London departments. He preferred the independent local administration of general laws. This preference is consistent with his powerful sense of community. But he had no qualms about the "extended action of law." He argued quite soberly that if we take men as we find them—which we must do—we cannot assume that the spontaneous actions of private individuals will produce the sort of society where everyone is adequately fed, housed, and educated. Not every man is motivated to do the best for himself let alone others.

A society in which the common good was promoted by spontaneous private action would be preferable to one where such an end was secured in part by public law. There is always a *prima facie* argument against constraint and compulsion of any sort, Green argued. As a medium of constraint, law is suspicious and its influence ought to be limited. But these limits cannot always be observed without risking unfair distribution of goods and services for many people: "If the ideal of true freedom is the maximum of power for all members of human society alike to make the best of themselves, we are right in refusing to ascribe the glory of freedom to a state in which the apparent elevation of the few is founded on the degradation of the many." (W.III.372) Law must intervene to restrict certain freedoms which promote inequality and social degradation. It cannot allow contracts of service whose outcome is the deterioration, physical and moral, of some of the parties.

It is difficult to determine either from the lecture on "Liberal Legislation" or the *Principles of Political Obligation* how extended the area of state action must be for Green. There were some matters which he felt had great priority, most notably, public education. On this issue, Green went much further than most of the liberals of his day in ascribing power to the machinery of law. On the issue of private property, however, Green's line was part of the "conventional wisdom." That is, he did not contest the accumulation of private wealth. But here, too, his remarks allow an interpretation which is consistent with a great amount of governmental interference. For instance, he writes, "The institution of property being only justifiable as a means to the free exercise of the social capabilities of all, there can be no true right to property of a kind which debars one class of men from such free exercise altogether." (W.III.372) In a capitalist economy a great many things have such a debarring effect, and a socialist could find in Green much theoretical support for the programs of a welfare state. The problem is that while Green advocates reform in specific areas, he does not specify in detail the role and the limits of state action. His ideal of self-realization and positive freedom for all is, on one interpretation, consistent with the most radical kind of reform. On the other hand, Green was always wary of legislation undertaken in advance of the existing "social sentiment."

There is in Green's advocacy of reform, and generally in his political theory, a tension between two ideals, both of which claimed his allegiance. These are the ideals of freedom and of community. But this tension, if it is a theoretical weakness, was also a source of strength in the man. In his day Green aligned himself with the right causes. Whether or not we would consider these causes radical enough today is another matter.

It might be an interesting exercise to try to determine which political and social programs Green would support were he alive today. If we were to do this we would have to bear in mind one principle which abided with Green throughout, namely, that all members of a society have an equal claim to the goods and services it offers. When this equality of rights is overriden, neither individual freedom nor the common good is secure. To promote this equality Green could consistently argue for public decision-making on a greater number of issues than most liberals of his day would allow. He concurred that the purpose of liberal legislation was to remove restrictions, and that the law was supposed to hinder the hindrances, but he had a much wider idea than other liberals of what constitutes a restriction and a hindrance. In this sense Green's views represent a significant departure from and advance upon the old liberalism.

Views on Education

When Green married in 1871 he also became a householder in the town of Oxford and was eligible to participate in the town's politics. In 1874 he was elected to the Oxford School Board and in 1876 he was elected by the North Ward as a representative to the Town Council. This was the first time a tutor of an Oxford college held the post of town councillor and Green's election contributed to bridging the gulf between the city and the University of Oxford. Nettleship tells us that the public project which most interested him as a town councillor was the building of a grammar school, or high school, for boys from the elementary schools of the town. He contributed money for the building and founded a yearly scholarship. It was the sort of school to fill the gap in middle-class education. The latter in England had become divorced from the universities and was considered second-rate. Throughout his career Green emphasized the necessity for eradicating social distinctions from the schools, for he viewed common education as a "true social leveller." (W.III.459)

It was privilege in all its forms, arbitrary exclusiveness, and inveterate snobbery that bothered Green most. As a student and a tutor at Oxford he had a handsome sampling of all these. Indeed, he felt that most of the institutions of higher learning in England were not only exclusive societies, they seemed to foster snobbery as well. While these institutions bred the English gentlemen who was supposed to be the "noblest work of God," Green remarked that "one gentleman makes many snobs." (M.cxi) One thing seemed clear to Green: there was no justification ever for the condescension evinced by members of privileged, educated classes toward those who had neither money nor education. While he was a tutor Green rarely expressed his personal political views, perhaps out of a respect for and desire to encourage independence of thought in his students. But he never allowed instances of either the snob mentality or condescension to pass without comment. When Bernard Bosanquet, who was his student, read an essay to him in which he argued for educational reforms as a precondition for the extension of the franchise, Green said simply: "If you imply that no one is fit to have a vote who has not had a university education, I don't agree with you."[12] This remark is all the more important in the light of Green's own efforts to reform education in England.

Apart from the fact that the universities were for a long time an Anglican monopoly—it was not until 1871 when the Universities Test Act became law that Dissenters of all creeds could get advanced degrees and fellowships, and Green, a Nonconformist, had to take the oath to the Thirty-Nine Articles of the Anglican Church in order to obtain his M.A. and a fellowship—sectarian instruction and other irrelevant criteria had produced a grading of the public schools which seemed to insulate the upper classes from the rest of the nation. According to Green, education was used almost like a political weapon to deepen the inevitable class distinctions. He confirmed this opinion after conducting his own investigations as assistant commissioner for the Schools Inquiry Commission established in December, 1864. The purpose of this commission was to investigate "the schools attended by the children of such of the gentry, clergy, professional and commercial men as are of limited means, and of farmers and tradesmen." (M.xiv) Green travelled to several parts of England talking to schoolmasters, observing schoolwork, calling on trustees and parents. His first headquarters was Birmingham, the constituency of John Bright. The men who were named commissioners with Green included Matthew Arnold and James Bryce. Their combined reports provided a severe indictment of the mid-Victorian schooling system. It was an exposition of the inadequacy of the schools, especially in the industrial centers of the nation, an inadequacy deriving from archaic teaching methods and curriculums, and wasted endowments.

In the official report he prepared for the commission, which many characterized as "stinging," as well as in a lecture "On the Grading of Secondary Schools," Green made a number of concrete recommendations, many of which were adopted in the program of the National Education League. The three points on which he insisted were "compulsory attendance, the maintenance of the schools out of the public funds and unsectarian instruction." (M.cxiii) Education and properly organized schools were for him one means of removing the barriers between classes of people: "Education endowments can be so worked as in some degree to efface the demarcations of class, to give a freedom of self-elevation on the social scale other than that given by money and to keep 'the career open to the talents.' " (M.lvii)

On the issue of the reorganization of schools Green offered more than vague, general guidelines. Having examined everything from the collapsing walls of school buildings to the often abysmal salaries of instructors, he accumulated facts and details which reveal a clearheaded view of what needed to be done. One of his most interesting proposals was the creation of graded secondary schools to serve the needs and interests of working- and middle-class children. The latter, confronted by the typical classics curriculum, poorly taught even at that, did not see that education was either essential or attractive. It was important, therefore, to establish a "ladder of learning" which would awaken the interest of the lower classes in learning and provide opportunities for humble boys to enter the universities. Green proposed that schools be graded according to the age to which education is continued as opposed to the prevailing system where grading was determined by the social position of the children attending the school. Grading according to age would in turn determine the type of subjects taught and the teaching methods employed. If a boy was to stop his education at the age of thirteen in order to enter his father's business, for instance, it was essential that he learn English grammar first and then if there was time and interest he might read the poetry of Homer. Those students who stayed on until they were eighteen and who could be induced to go to the university would have a different training.

The German model seemed more attractive to Green than the existing system in England. The former was based on a distinction between the "Gymnasium," which provided a classical education preparatory for university entry, and the "Real-Schule," which aimed to train students for various posts either in the civil service or in business. The main difference between the English and German systems as Green saw it was that the latter made a substantive distinction based on educational needs and interests whereas the former perpetuated social distinctions whereby schools provided either a "gentleman's education" or a middle-class education which was automatically graded as second-rate. In his lecture on "The Oxford High School for Boys," the school he did so much to found, he expressed his hope that the new school, in opening its doors to children of the working and lower middle classes, would contribute to the creation of an English society "in which all honest citizens will recognize themselves and be recognized by each other as gentlemen." (W.III.476)

Green's recommendations for educational reform called for the intervention of the state. He never wavered on the idea that there must be a law which made school attendance compulsory. On this matter he diverged from the entrenched voluntary principle of many Nonconformists. The prevailing view was that education, above all, must be free from governmental meddling, for the latter could only weaken the sense of parental obligation and undermine personal character. Green's own powerful adherence to the ideal of individual self-help and character improvement did not blind him, however, to the facts. The voluntary principle was "respectable" enough, but as far as education was concerned, "it did not square with the facts." (W.III.427) The plain truth was that those who most needed education were not in a position either to demand it or do anything about getting it. While Green recognized a presumption against state action wherever personal voluntary action was possible and effective, he advocated a state system of education and this he did in the name of social equality and justice.

Religion

Nettleship tells us that religion was the subject that "lay nearest" to Green's heart though he wrote very little on it. (M.xcii) Some of his lectures on parts of the New Testament are preserved, but these are not original contributions to biblical criticism. He expressed his personal convictions in two lay sermons delivered at Balliol in 1870 and 1877. In the "Witness of God" and "Faith" Green reveals a position considerably at variance with traditional Christian dogma. Faith is independent of historical evidence, he tells us. (W.III.261) People think their faith derives from their acceptance of certain events in the past. But the object of a Christian's belief is not, according to Green, the historical birth, death, and resurrection of Jesus. It is rather the living presence of God working in the individual. (W.III.263) To treat the spiritual life as other than the disposition of man's mind and character to seek unity with God, which is also a unity with oneself, is to fall into dogmatic theology. Green would have none of that "chain of reasoning." God communicates to man in many ways, for he is immanent in all of man's moral, artistic, and scientific endeavors. Indeed, to be conscious of God is to be conscious of an essential unity in reality. The various ways man exerts himself to achieve self-perfection is the best evidence of God's presence:

No eye can see or ear hear him. The assertion that he exists cannot be verified like any other matter of fact. But what if that be not because he is so far off, but because he is near? You cannot know him as you know a particular fact related to you, but neither can you so know yourself, and it is yourself, not as you are, but as in seeking him you become, that is his revelation. . . . "The word of God is very nigh thee, even in thy mouth and in thy heart." It is the word that

has been made man; that has been uttering itself in all the high en-
deavours, the long-suffering love, the devoted search for truth,
which have so far moralised mankind, and that now speaks in your
conscience. It is the God in you which strives for communication with
God. [W.III.272-73]

For Green, there is no fundamental antithesis between the
divine and the human, hence no mediation is required between God and man. "The sense of Sin," Green once remarked, "is very much an illusion."[13] This version of Christianity is strongly reminiscent of Origen, the early Eastern
Church Father who was later excommunicated for advocating
that all human beings must necessarily achieve salvation in virtue of their participation in the divine. Green's is a
philosophical sort of Christianity rather than a theological
one. While he used the language of Orthodox Christianity, he
did not expound a specific or traditional type of theology. He
had little interest in the orthodox-heterodox controversies,
and ultimately it made no difference to him what forms men
chose to worship God. The important thing was that people
have what he called "the root of the matter in them" and this
could not be identified with rituals or historical creeds. (M.c)

Personally, he had an aversion to Roman Catholicism, the
Anglican Church, and the monastic life, for these seemed to
him to place personal sanctity and salvation above man's duty
to his fellowmen. When the poet Gerard Manley Hopkins,
whom Green had tutored in philosophy, converted to Roman
Catholicism, Green wrote a letter to H. S. Holland in which he
characterized "saintliness" as an attitude, in effect a refined
form of self-indulgence: "I imagine him [Hopkins]—perhaps
uncharitably—to be one of those, like his ideal J. H. Newman,
who instead of opening themselves to the revelation of God in
the reasonable world, are fain to put themselves into an
attitude—saintly it is true, but still an attitude. True citizenship 'as unto the Lord' (which includes all morality) I reckon
higher than 'saintliness' in the technical sense."[14]

One could be just as selfish being a saint as a sinner, and if
one "hugged" one's personal sanctity there was nothing particularly elevating about that. In another letter he contrasts
the monastic forms of cooperation with secular forms evident
in the family and the state. He finds the former no longer rel-

evant or useful to society: "It does nothing to organize life," he writes. "The real movement of the world has passed it by." The weakness within monasticism as well as in ordinary religions whether Catholic or Protestant derived from a contrast on which religions have usually based both doctrine and ritual, namely, an "antithesis between Church and World, the religious and the secular."[15] It was Green's belief that mankind had gone beyond such an antithesis and its implications. He attributed this advance to the work of human reason. God was not merely a "sensual presence in the sacraments" but rather a pervading force in the organization of society. This force, evinced in the operation of man's rational faculty, informs and mobilizes the moral and social consciousness of man. The voice of God does not speak so much through the authoritative pronouncements of a priest but in the "educated conscience" of ordinary men.

A common thread underlies Green's criticism both of institutionalized religion and of the educational system in England. Both the church and the schools were protective and exclusive. Men in both spheres affected attitudes—personal sanctity on the one hand, snobbery on the other. Nettleship writes, "The enemy which he dreaded for religion was not either orthodoxy or unorthodoxy, but selfishness and indifference." (M.c) There were a number of ways in which one could insulate oneself from society; a misdirected religiosity was one of them.

The root of the matter for Green lay in the life of citizenship, in the individual's devotion to those communal efforts and ideals which make men better and bring the good life within the reach of all. To be a Christian is to be a conscientious citizen. Green's religion has been called a "civic one."[16] Scarcely the opium of the people, the religious life, if properly construed, was best evidenced in social action. Arguments about the compatibility of faith and reason were for Green beside the point. The need for making life better for all men, for fulfilling one's obligations to others and for working toward self-improvement, was not undermined by the findings of science. It was weakened by selfishness and indifference.

It may be asked to what extent Green himself was a Christian in the sense required by orthodox creeds. The question has been raised in the case of such diverse thinkers of the nineteenth century as Hegel and Kierkegaard. His biographer writes that "he cared about the reality of religion and not about its accessories, and was convinced that its reality does not depend upon its dogmatic expression." (M.c) That Green was deeply religious cannot be denied; that he was an orthodox Christian is not easy to say. He did not think that adoption of orthodox creeds was a necessary condition either for Christian prayer or for leading a Christian life. He wrote in a letter that religion and morality for him were identical insofar as one can adopt the moral point of view in a wholly religious way.[17] He conceived of his own interest in philosophy as religious in the sense "that it is . . . the reasoned intellectual expression of the effort to get to God."[18] The moral life then would consist of those actions and attitudes which evinced the presence of God in one, where this presence is construed as a consciousness by the individual of a self he strives to become.

Green's religious views provide a useful background to a basic theme in his moral and political philosophy: that moral effort is directed toward self-perfection, which necessarily includes the perfection of the society in which one lives. But it is terribly important to be clear about what Green had in mind when in the sermons on "Faith" and "Witness to God" he refers to the "moralising agent." A certain bifurcation between a "lower" and a "higher" self has been attributed to Green, and this it seems to me reduces his thesis to some of his less felicitous expressions, thus neglecting the whole of his argument. Green's idea that God is identical with the self of every man as realized in its possibilities, as somehow more perfect, and that it is the consciousness of such a self which reveals to man his duties toward society, does not commit him to a dualism between a higher, rational self and a lower, animal self. The man who is capable of moralizing himself and creating those conditions upon which cooperative life in society rests does not consist of two radically opposed selves. Rather, there are in man diverse wants and desires not all of whose realization conduces to a better life for the self and others. Green's distinctive thesis is that societies and their manifold institutions are founded not by the momentary wants and appetites of individuals but by ideas which men entertain, by ideals they project describing better ways of being. Society, he declares, "implies the action in man of a principle in virtue of which he projects himself into the future . . . as some more perfect being than he actually is, and thus seeks not merely to satisfy momentary wants but to become 'another man,' to become more nearly as this more perfect being. Under this influence wants and desires that have their root in the animal nature become an impulse of improvement . . . which forms, enlarges, and re-casts societies; always keeping before man in various guise . . . an unrealized ideal of a best." (W.III.269-70)

The fact that the phrase "another man" is enclosed in quotation marks indicates that Green is not advancing a form of Pauline dualism. Moreover, animal wants need not be eradicated. Indeed, they cannot be. What occurs in the moralization process, in the effort toward self-perfection, is the creative assertion of a practical reason upon the desiring consciousness. This is a condition for moral action which, according to Green, "begins from ideas." (W.III.235) Moral action then presupposes both deliberation and the projection of ideals, not the rejection of a lower self. Indeed, the main contrast in Green's ethics is between the realization of partial aspects of the self and the realization of the self as a whole. This is the theme of the following chapter and, as we shall see, the idea is not without its own difficulties. But one of the problems does not happen to be a dualism between a lower and a higher self.

On this score, Green's moral philosophy has been travestied by readings which seem to be the result of a rather odd and wholly contemporary inability to ascribe any meaning to the phrase "becoming a better person" without appealing to a moral dualism. What Green was getting at, however, would have been understood easily by Aristotle. The latter was no dualist.

The main emphasis in Green's self-realization ethics is on a kind of religious conscientiousness which is effective in this world, a conscientiousness aroused as much by love as by a sense of duty. It is a conscientiousness best construed in a teleological rather than a deontological sense. His religious views give us the right to say of Green's moral ideal that it enjoins action not for the sake of obedience to a categorical imperative but for the achievement of the good life for all men.

We shall pursue this idea further in the next chapter.

Death

Green died prematurely from blood poisoning in 1882, leaving most of his written work unfinished to be edited by his students and friends. His upbringing in Evangelicalism and the fact that the England of his day derived its moral and social tone from religious faith and observance have no doubt contributed to the view that his religious and moral ideas are now of historical interest at best. But on such concerns as form the subject matter of a religious or moral philosophy it is terribly difficult to decide what is of merely historical rather than enduring interest. What seems more clear is that it was not Green's aim to provide his fellowmen with a strong ethical uplift or to turn his students into prigs. This rather uncharitable view of Green expressed by C. D. Broad is contradicted by the words of Green's great adversary and probably his most astute critic, Henry Sidgwick:

Though without fame, he had no envy. But he had a strong realism. He saw what it is considered cynical to see—the absurdities of many persons, the pomposities of many creeds, the splendid zeal with which missionaries rush on to teach what they do not know, the wonderful earnestness with which most incomplete solutions of the universe are thrust upon us as complete and satisfying.[19]

The relationship between Thomas Hill Green and Henry Sidgwick is a salutary example of what is missing most in philosophical dialogue today. Although Green and Sidgwick disagreed on practically every philosophical issue, their critical reviews of each other's work were not marred by offensive witticisms. They did not write for victory or to set conceptual traps for opponents. They respected each other. Green was especially sensitive to how easily one might substitute mere cleverness for genuine philosophical criticism and insight. This attitude may account for the uniform dullness of his writings. The spirit in which both Green and Sidgwick wrote, however, reveals the highest sort of commitment to philosophy and the deepest concern for the well-being of man.

CHAPTER 3

Self-Realization Ethics

Green thought it important to ask, "Why rights at all?" This is a question about "grounds," a query into the reasons why claims and powers to act are, or ought to be, allowed as *rights* so to act. According to Green, the ground of actual rights is to be found in "an end to which the maintenance of rights contributes." (23LP) The reason why certain powers should be secured to individuals as rights "lies in the fact that these powers are necessary to the fulfillment of man's vocation as a moral being." (23LP) Rights are the claims of a human moral capacity, a capacity "without which a man would not be a man." (30LP) The idea implicit in the classical theory of natural rights that one need only be a man in order to have rights is potentially misleading for Green unless one clearly indicates that "being a man" means possessing moral personality and moral purpose in some sense. It is only among persons, in the ethical sense of "person," that rights can exist. (25LP) To justify rights is to show how and why they are required by the moral person. The idea is that a person cannot develop or realize his moral capacity unless he has rights. And since a man cannot be a man unless this capacity is developed, rights are necessary: "There ought to be rights because the moral personality . . . ought to be developed and it is developed through rights." (26LP)

The core of Green's theory of rights derives from a certain moral psychology and a conception of a moral ideal or moral end. He argues that human beings possess what he calls "moral personality" and that there is a peculiarly human goal to whose achievement rights contribute. What, however, does Green mean by such terms as "moral personality" and "moral capacity"? How does he conceive of the moral end to which he supposes all rights are relative? We will examine some answers to these questions here and in the ensuing chapter.

49

At the basis of Green's moral psychology and ethical theory is a distinctive conception of the self and human action. Green developed his theory of the self in opposition to what he took to be the "popular philosophy" of his day, in effect the psychology, epistemology, and moral theory of the great British empiricists from Hobbes down to John Stuart Mill. What was at stake in Green's criticism of the received view of the self was the autonomy of the individual as well as the autonomy of the subject matter of moral philosophy. The conceptual framework of naturalism had, according to Green, reduced both the individual and the sort of judgments the latter makes which are called "moral."

Green devoted a good part of his lectures and writing to a critical review of certain theories. In a short essay entitled "Popular Philosophy in its Relation to Life" (W.III.92-115), he comments on what he considers the main points in the moral psychology of Hobbes, Locke, and Hume. Some of Green's remarks are perceptive; sometimes the charges he brings against the empiricists are simpleminded. The correctness of Green's criticism, however, is not the issue here. Its value lies in the clues it provides for an understanding of his own ideas.

He attacks first the psychology of Hobbes. There is, Green observes, an inconsistency in the *homo homini lupus* image of man which Hobbes projects. This image is based on a purely naturalistic account of human wants and drives in which man's appetites are likened to those of the wolf. But, "the wolf eats when he is hungry and has done with it" (W.III.97) whereas man, on Hobbes's own admission, is a self-interested calculator of ways and means to accumulate power and pleasure. Green concurs with Hobbes that man has animal appetites, but a simple parallel between these and the appetites of a wolf will not do. Hobbes wants to stress the natural origins of human wants and drives. Green's point is that to get as much as one can for oneself, to seek power for oneself, is not a strictly wolfish or animal appetite but a peculiarly human appetite. Such an appetite, not wholly explicable in naturalistic terms, is at work even in the state of nature which Hobbes describes. Green writes: "With Hobbes, the feeling on which morality rests is the mere animal appetite, the sense of want, with the impulse to appropriate that which will satisfy the want. The appetite, however, has to lose its merely animal character before it will account even for the state of universal warfare in which, according to Hobbes, society begins."(W.III.97) Hobbes can argue that the social and moral enterprise originates from the transformation of animal appetite into deliberate self-interest and that it is the latter which is the source of the idea of duty and the moral sentiments. Green's rejoinder then is that neither Hobbes nor Locke nor Hume later on can explain how such transformation takes place given the separation which these writers presuppose between feeling and thought. Such separation is at the basis of empiricist psychology. It is expressed in Hume's famous remark, "Reason is and ought to be the slave of the passions."

If one begins with man the creature, possessed solely of animal wants and drives, a *tabula rasa,* a bundle of sensations and emotions, one cannot get very far in explaining how it is that he achieves conceptual knowledge and creates the myriad world of art, religion, science, and morality. Where man's reason is viewed as essentially passive, emerging only to combine various sensations or to calculate means for the achievement of more pleasurable feelings, what we arrive at is certainty with respect to private mental states on the one hand —this is as far as man's knowledge can go—and a world of prudential calculating machines on the other hand—this is as far as man's morality and social effort can go. A psychology which posits man as solely a calculator aiming at self-preservation and the maximization of pleasure, moved primarily by considerations of self-love with a limited disinterested benevolence, whose adherence to a social and moral code derives from certain natural sympathies and fears and nothing else—such is the psychology Green attributes to the empiricists—cannot account for the phenomena of moral experience.

What are these phenomena, according to Green? Well, for one thing, human beings make all sorts of judgments in which they praise some actions and condemn others; furthermore, they ascribe responsibility even apart from a legal framework. It seems also to be a fact that they view themselves as having obligations to perform certain actions as opposed to merely being obliged to do something, and that these actions very frequently have little to do with the achievement of personal pleasure. Finally, human beings do relate to and cooperate with each other in ways which reveal a great capacity for acting solely on the basis of other-regarding interests. These facts are of interest to the moral philosopher, and it is his task to decide what they are all about. But a purely naturalistic and deterministic ethics based on psychological egoism reduces these facts and assimilates the subject matter of moral philosophy to physiology and anthropology. This reduction makes a travesty of man's moral sense, Green would say; for this sense is taken to be a purely natural appetite or aversion, and the moral development of man is no more than a historical record of likes and dislikes.

What is missing in the great empiricists and the philosophers of naturalism, according to Green, is the awareness that man, unlike other forms of life, is self-conscious. This fact means among other things that he can detach himself from nature: "Unless man had consciously detached himself from nature, no 'Treatise of Human Nature' could have been written. He would not be trying to account to himself for his own moral life, even by reducing it to a natural one; would not be asking what nature is to him or he to nature, if he were merely the passive receptacle of natural impressions, and not at the same time constructive and free."(W.III.112)

For Green, the enterprises of knowledge and morality presuppose the active exercise of human reason. His main quarrel with his illustrious predecessors in English philosophy focuses on the secondary role they ascribe to reason and the consequent failure to realize that it is in virtue of his rational and essentially social nature and not his mere animal appetites whether for food or pleasure that man has come to moralize himself and his institutions. Both in the moral judgments he makes as well as in his claims to knowledge man is going beyond "mere nature" and evinces the constructive exercise of his reason. The difference between Green and the naturalists lies in what each side takes the "given" to be: i.e., the material of which we have knowledge and the area within which man exerts moral effort.

Following Kant, Green argues that with respect to what man claims to know, "he goes beyond sense as much when he pronounces that he can only know things individual, or phenomena, as when he claims to know substances and the universal"; for the world out there is not merely given to man's sensing, "it is traversed by the currents of his intellect." (W.III.95) The material of which we may be said to have knowledge is organized into an order of knowable facts by the operation of what Green calls a "self-distinguishing consciousness." (52PE) Green does not deny the importance of sensation in the acquisition of knowledge: "We do not dispute the validity of Locke's challenge to a man by any amount of thinking to produce a single 'simple idea' to himself. We admit that mere thought can no more produce the facts of feeling, than mere feeling can generate thought. But we deny that there is really such a thing as 'mere feeling' or 'mere thought.' " (51PE) Green subscribed to the Kantian doctrine that "the understanding makes nature"; the categories of pure reason are presupposed in all experience. But he also insisted that, for human beings at least, no separation could be made between feeling or sensation, and thought. Other animals feel but do not think. For the experiencing human, however, feeling and thought are inseparable in the presence of a world of phenomena. The mutual interplay of sensation and reason or of feeling and thought "creates" the phenomena as knowable facts.

When Green asserts that the knowledge of nature cannot itself be "a part or product of nature" (8PE), he means that the reasoning faculty unifies and coordinates the diverse material of sensation and perception and confers upon them the status of "facts" or "objects of experience." Knowledge is of these facts and is therefore beyond mere sensation. But Green did not remain with the restriction Kant had placed upon his own dictum that the understanding makes nature. Kant maintained that man cannot know the "things-in-themselves" which are the source of sensation and perception. He ascribed an independent reality to the *ding-an-sich* or thing-in-itself; Green questioned this separation.

In Book I of the *Prolegomena* he outlines a metaphysics of knowledge where he conceives of nature as constituted by a spiritual principle in virtue of which it exhibits a unity. Everything in nature is to be understood as existing in and through definite relations: "We can attach no meaning to 'reality,' as applied to the world of phenomena, but that of existence under definite and unalterable relations; and we find that it is only for a thinking consciousness that such relations can subsist." (51PE) The various connections and sequences which exist in nature are made possible by an all-uniting, divine consciousness. This consciousness permeating man enables the latter to know the world of nature. According to Green, the unity in nature implies that man's knowledge is not the product of two separate sources as Kant supposed, namely, things-in-themselves and the understanding. Everything is pervaded by a spiritual principle which includes man as knowing and feeling and nature as known. The assertion, then, that man's knowledge is not a part or product of nature comes to mean further for Green that human understanding is itself a product of a divine or spiritual consciousness.

The insistence upon a spiritual principle pervading nature in virtue of which man is something more than a bundle of mere animal appetites and consecutive sensations is perhaps the most difficult and least acceptable of Green's metaphysical doctrines. It is doubtful that this principle represents an advance upon Kant as Green thought. Moreover, it appears to commit one to treating human beings as though they were radically different from other species in ways which cannot be specified in comprehensible terms. Green did believe that a moral theory presupposes some metaphysical view of man and a sound epistemology, and he was probably correct in his belief. It is not clear, however, that he succeeded in formulating either a workable metaphysics or epistemology. Indeed, as has been noted by critics sympathetic to Green, he made far more sense when he analyzed the moral experience of men than when he theorized about a spiritual consciousness. Moreover, it does seem true that one can readily accept a unity of thought and feeling as characteristic of man's moral effort without grounding this unity in some divine principle. If Green was concerned to explain the conditions of human moralization because he felt that the received philosophy was most inadequate on this score, he could have proceeded to do so without postulating a divine principle. Many later critics both of psychological egoism and hedonistic utilitarianism were to advance their arguments in terms descriptive of human as opposed to divine endeavor. It is possible, then, to review both Green's criticism of the moral psychology of utilitarianism and his own recommendations apart from his metaphysics. This we will do in the sections that follow.

For Green, the most unsettling aspect in the received theory of morals was its emphasis on feeling, or the passions. The motive for imputable action was conceived as a simple desire for pleasure or for agreeable states of mind. The desire for pleasure was supposed to be the source of moral action on the one hand, while providing the content of a moral ideal on the other. Actions were viewed either as virtuous or vicious according to whether they produced pleasure or pain. One of the main points in Green's criticism of psychological hedonism is that this hedonism makes it difficult to speak of the idea of duty as a possible motive for action or as providing a restraint upon action. (W.III.109) A psychological hedonist can admit that man fulfills his obligations and indeed that he ought to do so, but the reason for this is that meeting one's obligations ensures a good reputation and this is a source of pleasure. To treat the "I ought" in these terms, however, is, according to Green, to reduce the sense of obligation and conscience to pleasurable sensations. It is a reduction which further can lead to moral peril. A moral theory based upon psychological hedonism can, at times, approve of actions which most of us ordinarily would find repugnant and prohibitive. Most of us, as Green saw it, do find ourselves disapproving of certain actions which, though they may produce pleasurable states of mind in some, are yet wholly at variance with what we take to be morally fitting and proper.

Green's adverse criticism of hedonism aimed to show that self-love and the desire for pleasure are not the mainspring of human action. In his moral activity, in performing those actions which can be judged either praiseworthy or blameworthy, a human being, for Green, is not motivated by simple animal impulse transformed into deliberate self-interest, but by a complex interplay of desire, will, and intellect in the pursuit of what he takes to be some good for the self as a whole. This good is not to be construed as pleasure. Pleasure, Green argued, is not properly speaking an object of action but a feeling which may accompany the completion of an action. He conceived the object of morally imputable action in terms of self-realization.

The idea that the individual has a unified self in virtue of which we can attribute to him a moral personality and a moral capacity is the distinctive thesis in Green's moral psychology. In various sections of the *Prolegomena* he characterizes the self as a conscious unity of feelings, desires, and thoughts. The ego is an "all-uniting, self-seeking, self-realizing subject." (99PE) If we can overcome our contemporary aversion to some of Green's linguistic mumbo-jumbo and allow him a hearing, we may be able to get to the heart of his idea of what it means to be a person and therefore a subject of rights. We have to remember that he was primarily concerned to outline a moral psychology which allows for the pertinence of moral categories and judgments.

According to Green, moral conduct—conduct to which moral predicates typically apply—implies motivated action as opposed to instinctive behavior. A motive is the "idea of an end, which a self-conscious subject presents to itself, and which it strives and tends to realize." (87PE) Of course, certain elementary motives are sometimes indistinguishable from animal appetites and wants. But no motive proper can be reduced to an instinct. A basic want or drive becomes a motive, Green says, when "upon the want there supervenes the presentation of the want by a self-conscious subject to himself, and with it the self-satisfaction to be attained in the filling of the want." (88PE) What makes an action a distinctly *human* action is the fact that it is motivated; and while motives may originate in natural wants or animal appetites, they are not reducible to the latter. The existence of motives implies self-consciousness on the one hand and the idea of objects whose achievement will yield self-satisfaction on the other. Hunger is not, strictly speaking, a motive and, even though we achieve satisfaction upon eating, eating is not the sort of action in the performance of which we are made morally better or worse.

At the basis of Green's moral psychology is the distinction he makes between motived action and impulsive, or instinctive, behavior. He notes that the difference cannot always be verified empirically, especially in the case of other persons. In our own case, through introspection, we are better able to tell whether we have acted on impulse or on a motive we can specify. The important point is that the presence of a motive and what might be called a "thought-dependent" desire renders an action imputable. Furthermore, in all action which is motivated, whether this action is judged good or bad, the object which an individual aims to achieve is conceived of as a personal good: "The motive in every imputable act, for which the agent is conscious on reflection that he is answerable, is a desire for a personal good in some form or other." (91PE)

On what principle does Green distinguish motived action from instinctive behavior, desire from mere impulse? The whole burden of his argument seems to derive from the distinctly human fact of self-consciousness. A mere want or urge which is something that occurs *in me* becomes a motive when, through the operation of self-conscious thought, I become aware that the object I seek is one *I* have posited, is something *I* want. The point seems to be that the self is the source of motives and desires which form the content of one's will in a way in which it is not the author of mere impulses and animal urges. In instances of desiring and willing strictly so called, there is, Green says, "a desire in which the man enacts himself, as distinct from one which acts upon him." (146PE) Self-consciousness then refers to more than just the rational faculty of man. It is that peculiar capacity in man in virtue of which he can present his feelings to himself and at the same time distinguish himself from them. (120PE) Moreover, to be self-conscious is to be aware that the self is a unity of desires, feelings, and intellect. These are components of the self, but the self is not a mere bundle of these and is not reducible to any combination of these. The ego is irreducible and the self as a whole has in Green's account an object whose achievement is satisfying.

Green's analysis requires that we ask ourselves whenever we are pursuing any goal or entertaining a certain desire whether the fulfillment of this desire or the achievement of the particular goal will benefit our *real* selves or our selves as a whole. A common but mistaken view of Green's thesis is that he distinguished between an animal self and a real, rational self. This interpretation has misdirected readings of Green's political philosophy and specifically his conception of freedom. Actually, for Green the most important fact about the human self is its unity, and the distinctions he draws do not require a bifurcation of the individual. He does not deny the reality of animal appetites and needs which are independent of self-consciousness. He maintains rather that such desires as those for food are not elements in our moral experience. His argument is directed to an analysis of man's *moral* experience, and for him a key element in this experience is the self conceived of as a unity. The real self is not a reified entity shorn of animal urges but what he calls the "self-as-a-whole." In virtue of his capacity to desire objects that satisfy the self-as-a-whole and to pursue goals that reflect the unity of the self, man is a proper subject for moral analysis. Again, lest we confuse matters, Green is not saying that we always in fact desire objects that satisfy the self as a whole. Only when we do in fact so desire and proceed to satisfy such a desire can we be judged morally. This is the force of Green's various statements to the effect that the "quest of self-satisfaction is the form of all moral activity." (160PE)

Such remarks have provoked the charge of egoism against Green's ethics. But a more than cursory reading of the *Prolegomena* will convince the reader that Green is scarcely propounding an egoistic ethics. Nor must the use of the word "satisfaction" mislead the reader into thinking that he is advancing a version of hedonism. The thesis that desire in those actions which are morally accountable is always for a personal good does not imply that the agent is seeking to achieve a state which affects or benefits primarily himself. "Personal" in Green's ethics has the force of "self-conscious" and "self-referent."[1] The object is something the self wants and it may in many cases have to do with the well-being of someone else. Moreover, the terms "good" and "satisfaction" do not mean pleasure. Green agreed with Butler and others that an individual pursues specifiable objects and not something vague called "pleasure." The fact that we experience a feeling of pleasure when we do achieve what we have been aiming at is no ground for believing that the achievement of pleasure provides the main motive for our actions. The quest for self-satisfaction may be evinced in a number of different ways, which range from the "enjoyment of pleasure" at one end to the "more heroic forms of self-sacrifice" and "fulfillment of a universal practical law" on the other. (159-60PE)

The charge of hedonism cannot be brought against Green's thesis, but we can raise other questions. Setting aside for the moment what "self-satisfaction" or "self-realization" amounts to as a moral ideal, we should ask what Green has in mind when he refers to the self as a whole. What is the "whole self" supposed to be contrasted with? What does the "unity" of the self refer to?

The unity of the individual self is probably the central thesis in the moral psychology of self-realization ethics. In the words of a contemporary exponent, "The unity of persons is their most distinctive characteristic, that without which they would not be moral selves at all; and experiences, acts . . . and states of affairs have moral significance only in relation to such unities."[2] This is a fair statement of Green's view as well. But it is important to try to specify the unitary character of the self.

The theory of desire and the relation between desire, intellect, and will presented in Book II of the *Prolegomena* suggests some answers. Green traces the self's unity to the manner in which we attend to our various desires. He writes: "We are apt to speak of our desires for this object or that as if each operated on us singly, or as if each had its effect on us independently of the others. . . . But such language is not a true expression of our experience. We are never so exclusively possessed by the desire for any object as to be quite unaffected by the thought of other desired objects, of which we are conscious that the loss or gain would have a bearing on our happiness." (127PE) According to Green, our awareness that the satisfaction or frustration of one desire bears on that of others is a consequence of our ability to detach ourselves from this or that desire and view ourselves as one subject whose fulfillment and happiness are dependent upon the satisfaction of many different desires. This is as true of "the man of most concentrated purpose" as it is of men with less concentrated direction, "who live with more divided aims." (128PE)

The various desires of the self, then, constitute a unity in the sense that they are desires of a self who is aware of them all. "Unity" does not necessarily imply harmony, although Green sometimes seems to bypass the reality of conflict between desires, especially when he argues that a person who is experiencing such a conflict does not desire any one particular object at all. (138PE) He does not deny that we often desire objects which we recognize to be incompatible with each other, which satisfy at best only partial aspects of the self. He maintains rather that when an individual is in a divided state, when "conflicting passions are striving for mastery within him," it cannot be said that he is desiring in the same sense as when he finally opts for one particular object: "The object of his final pursuit is one which he desires in the sense that for the time he identifies himself with it." (138PE) Green seems to distinguish between different "levels" of desiring, and he argues as though conflict occurs on one level only, namely, where the self has not yet exerted itself to choose one way or another. When an individual finally "makes up his mind," the dominant desire reflects his conscious, deliberate choice, and the object of this desire is conceived of as good for the self as a whole. This means that for the time being the chosen pursuit is wholly satisfying, all desires and interests of the self having been taken into account.

The unitary character of the self then may be explicated in the first place in terms of a unity among the diverse desires of the self. This unity in turn is a function of the fact that all these desires claim our attention at some time or another. These desires have a common ground insofar as they impinge upon each other and no *one* desire ever possesses us to the exclusion of other desires. It would follow, we may suppose, for Green, that if we are ever so "possessed," we are not, strictly speaking, desiring at all.

There is, however, another kind of unity evidenced in the human personality. Insofar as desire for anything is "more than an indefinite yearning for we know not what," it "involves an employment of the understanding." (134PE) Green argues that there is a symmetry between desiring and thinking in that neither can operate without involving the other. Whenever it can be said of a man that he is pursuing some end, whether the object is the enjoyment of a sensual pleasure or the solution of a mathematical problem, there is some mutual involution of desire and understanding. A good summary of Green's view is the following passage:

... our conclusion must be that there is really a single subject or agent, which desires in all the desires of a man, and thinks in all his thoughts, but that the action of this subject as thinking—thinking speculatively or understanding, as well as thinking practically—is involved in all desires, and that its action as desiring is involved in all its thought. Thus thought and desire are not to be regarded as separate powers, of which one can be exercised by us without, or in conflict with, the other. They are rather different ways in which the consciousness of self ... expresses itself. [136PE]

There is no such thing as passionless intellect or mindless desire according to Green. The unity of the self further implies, then, that the faculties of man do not function independently of one another. We do not simply desire or just think or merely will when we perform actions for which we are morally accountable. We do all three at once, especially when we are pursuing what we take to be a good for the self as a whole.

The main contrast, the important conflict in man's moral experience, as Green saw it, does not lie in the supposed antagonism between a man's desires and his cool thoughts but, as one writer put it, "between the conceived good of the self *as a whole* and the conceived good of *partial aspects* of the self."[3] This conflict is the source of the moral "ought." According to Green, morally obligatory conduct is action which is conducive to self-realization. This has the force of the moral "ought," of Kant's categorical imperative. It is not simply a prudential "ought," because on Green's conception of the "good of the self as a whole" taken as the moral ideal, the good of the self emerges as a common or social good. The action it makes obligatory is far from being egoistic; it is mainly altruistic. Green can equate self-realization with the ideal of a common good because he maintains that among the desires and interests of the self taken as a unity there are needs for social cooperation and natural fellow-feelings, that is, desires for the well-being of others. In the chapters that follow we will note how "being moral" for Green implies acting in ways that are predominantly other-directed.

In virtue, then, of the unitary character of the self, a human being seeks self-satisfaction or self-realization. This is the goal of motivated human action. It is not the satisfaction of all desires, however, that serves the interest of the self as a whole. There are desires whose fulfillment satisfies only partial aspects of the self; this constitutes self-satisfaction in one sense. But this satisfaction is not the self-realization which Green takes to be a *moral* goal. The achievement of the moral goal of self-realization requires the satisfaction of those desires which represent the interests of the self as a whole.

Now we may ask, how, according to Green, do we choose among our various desires? How do we know in advance which set of satisfactions will yield the good of the self as a whole? Intuitively it would seem that we cannot always tell except in gross cases. The case Green most frequently refers to is that of the "habitual toper." The latter obviously is indulging a partial aspect of himself and in so doing is letting his other needs and interests fall by the wayside. His is a typical case of wrongdoing on two counts: he harms himself in attending to one limited "side" of himself, and he harms others insofar as he does not meet his obligations. In this instance a very strong desire does not happen to be one whose fulfillment serves the end of self-realization. In discussing the example of the alcoholic, Green argues against treating the strength of a desire as a criterion for the desirability of its satisfaction. If we are going to try to make sense of what "self-realization" amounts to, it is important to determine whether there are any ways of evaluating our desires.

One sympathetic critic of Green has urged that there are two assignable characteristics which may serve as criteria for evaluating the status of desires. Campbell appeals to the self which exhibits "a 'lateral' as well as a 'longitudinal' unity." It is worthwhile quoting the relevant passage in full:

The self is aware of itself as a being which persists as a relatively permanent identity throughout all the successive changes of life. It is natural, therefore, that the self should regard an interest or desire of a relatively permanent nature as being, *ceteris paribus,* more authentically representative of itself than one which is relatively transient. In the second place, the unity of which the self is conscious . . . is, as it were, a "lateral" as well as a "longitudinal" unity, a unity comprehending contemporaneous, as well as successive, differences. It is natural, therefore, that the self should regard interests or desires of a relatively comprehensive nature—"broad" interests, like those in raising a family . . . which spread over a wide span of experience, informing well-nigh the whole content of personality—as being more authentically representative of the self than interests or desires of a relatively narrow compass.[4]

These words of a contemporary writer reflect the main trend in Green's moral psychology. Green also argues that desires which are relatively permanent and comprehensive are the ones whose satisfaction is conducive to self-realization. In effect the existence of such desires renders the phrase "self as a whole" meaningful. Moreover, in the pursuit of their satisfaction the individual evinces his peculiarly moral personality and moral capacity.

Admittedly the criteria of relative permanence and comprehensiveness are vague, and in the literature of normative ethical theory the concept of self-realization is notoriously obscure. It seems true, after all, that a man can develop in a number of different ways satisfying a number of different desires or diverse interests. How are we to determine that he has realized or fulfilled himself or satisfied the interests of the self as a whole when he develops in one way rather than another? Does Green ultimately mean that the "realized self" is the morally conscientious and resolute self? Is the pursuit of self-realization finally and solely a dominant interest in developing a Kantian good will? These questions have been raised by many students of Green's *Prolegomena*, and it is important to decide how Green conceived of the moral end, or the *summum bonum*, for this concept will enable us to determine the sense in which moral personality is a condition for the ascription of rights and obligations.

A common interpretation of Green's view of the moral end or moral ideal is that it is a straightforward Kantian conception. Henry Sidgwick was the first critic to note that Green presents two views of the moral ideal and that he wavers between a narrower and a wider conception. In the wide view the "true good" of man is self-realization; in the narrow view it is virtue or the good will. According to Sidgwick, Green adheres to the narrow view insofar as he wants to hold that the true good is a common good.[5] More recently it has been argued that Green opts for the narrower view because his adherence to the essentials of Kantian ethics was unwavering. On this reading, to realize the capabilities of the self which Green takes to be the moral end of man is really "to achieve greater moral resolution, a completer subjection of the will to ethical ends."[6] The "moral capacity" to which Green alludes in the *Lectures* is really, then, a capacity simply to abide by the dictates of the moral law. It is the capacity to do one's duty as this is defined by the categorical imperative. In this interpretation rights are a condition for morally conscientious action. We need rights in order to obey the categorical imperative.

This, however, is a reduction of Green's view which does less than justice to his conception of the moral ideal and his notion of rights. It is true that Green adopted some concepts of Kant, but it is also true that he finally departed from the latter to develop the view that moral goodness is a function not merely of the good will but of the active pursuit of objects and ends which are considered ingredients in the good life. There is evidence in Green's work to support the view that the "perfection of being," as he frequently characterizes the *summum bonum,* is a perfection not in the narrow sense of virtuous character but in the wider sense of the development of human capacities.

Green accepted Kant's dictum, and it is true that he refers to the moral end sometimes in terms of a good or devoted will and sometimes in terms of self-realization. But it is a mistake to suppose that Green wavered between two *ends* from which he finally chose one. Actually, for Green, the good will as Kant conceived of it is not an "end" at all. As the *summum bonum,* the end is a particular form of life, and constitutent elements in this life are moral goodness or the good will *and* the realization of human capabilities. The good life is not defined solely in terms of moral conscientiousness. The good will is the "inner" side of morality; the realization of human capabilities is the ideal viewed from the "outer," or visible, side. For Green, both are elements in the good life.

In the interpretation I am recommending, the moral capacity is a capacity for achieving the good life, not simply a capacity for obeying the rules. This capacity, "without which a man would not be a man," as Green says, is an ability to posit and pursue ends, have and promote interests, fulfill purposes, and realize personal ideals. If we may borrow a term from Aristotle, it is a capacity for *eudaimonia.* Man's vocation as a moral being is a vocation to realize himself, "to make the most and best of humanity in his own person and in the persons of others." (244PE) Rights are required by *this* vocation.

We should look to the *Prolegomena* for an elucidation of the view here attributed to Green. It should be noted at this point that all talk about the good life as an end of man is vague, and Green is the first to admit this. It is, he says, almost impossible to define the perfectly good life until it is achieved. One can only have a "working" theory of it. (354PE)

In the first place, then, how does Green conceive of the Kantian good will? "The good will," he writes, "may be taken to mean a will possessed by some abstract idea of goodness or of moral law; and, if such possession were possible at all, except perhaps during moments of special spiritual detachments from the actualities of life, it would amount to a paralysis of the will for all effectual application to great objects of human interest." (247PE) If this is what Kant meant by the good will, then, according to Green, it cannot be the will of the good worker, the good citizen, the good father, all of whom, however, can be said to possess a good will. These people are good not primarily because they are acting in obedience to a moral law but because they are pursuing interests and achieving goals which happen to be worthwhile. They are interested in some form of "true well-being." (235PE)

Now, Green insists, a condition for the achievement of "true well-being" is a genuine interest in its achievement. The mark of the good worker, father, and citizen is a "governing interest or will" in human perfection. (247PE) It is in this sense that Green understands the "good will." It is a will not merely to moral goodness but to goodness of all sorts—intellectual, artistic, technical, and the rest. If the formation of such a will is taken to be an end of moral effort, it must be understood not as a will "determined merely by an abstract idea of law, but as implying (what in fact it must imply) a whole world of benefi-

cent social activities, which it shall sustain and coordinate."
(288PE)

Green thus deviates from a strict Kantian position and develops a teleological theory of the good strongly reminiscent
of Aristotle. He finds that Artistotle has offered the best account of man's true good, which he reiterates as follows: "The
full exercise or realization of the soul's faculties in accordance
with its proper excellence, which [is] an excellence of thought,
speculative and practical." (254PE) According to Aristotle, the
good men pursue is *eudaimonia,* or well-being. Well-being, or a
form of life in which men realize their capacities and goals, is
the *summum bonum* for Green as well.

Whether or not the good life is possible here on earth,
whether or not we can know finally in what human perfection
consists, it is still true to say, according to Green, that we are
activated by such an ideal. He believed that history provides
evidence for the pervasiveness in the minds and hearts of men
of a conception of human perfection and the good life. His
theory of moral progress committed him to the belief that
there is always an increase in the range of self-realization:
"The realization of human capacities has, in fact, taken a far
wider range with us than in the most advanced of ancient
states . . . every progress achieved opens up a further vista of
possibilities still unrealized." (257PE)

Green has been criticized for his naïve view of moral progress. No further comment is required on this. What is important to note, for our purpose, is that he conceived of this
progress in terms of self-realization, or the development of
human capabilities, and not in terms of "greater moral resolution." Moreover, the fact that he refers to the "range" of self-
realization suggests that he conceived of this in essentially
dynamic terms. Throughout the *Prolegomena* he notes that
one's picture of the "realized self," or of human perfection,
changes with the times. The moral ideal "is an idea, if the expression may be allowed, which gradually creates its own filling." (241PE) The objects and the various ends which are
pursued in an effort to achieve the good life vary both in history and in individual persons. (235PE) What a man will do to
achieve well-being depends very much on the circumstances in
which he finds himself and on his personal interests and

idiosyncracies: "The thought of his well-being will be to him the thought of himself as living in the successful pursuit of various interests . . . ranging, perhaps, from provision for his family to the improvement of public health or to the production of a system of philosophy." (234PE)

The philosopher, according to Green, cannot decide in advance in what "true well-being" consists. Thus, he cannot dictate actual duties and rights. He can only show that whatever rules are or ought to be acknowledged, whatever ends are or ought to be pursued, are those which contribute to the good life. Green's point is that no moral rule (except the rules or principles of justice) and no system of rights and duties contains the grounds of its rightness within itself. It is only by reference to an ideal of the good life that moral rules are obligatory and personal ends are desirable: "The effects of actions, institutions, etc., are to be valued according to their relation to the production of personal excellence." (355PE)

Green's conception of the *summum bonum* is probably no more and no less "adequate" than that of other philosophers. Whether we describe the ultimate end in terms of happiness as Mill does, or in terms of self-realization and human perfection as Green does, we are still left with the gnawing feeling that very little has been said. Green, like others, does not overcome what may be called the "occupational hazards" of the moral philosopher. What we should note here is simply that he departs significantly from the Kantian position and conceives of the moral life and morality in terms of the pursuit of ideals rather than as a conformity to moral rules. For Green, morality—being moral—is both the pursuit of ends and the observance of rules—activity in accordance with virtue. The moral agent is not to be identified solely with the morally conscientious fellow. The moral capacity is the capacity to choose things and do things and project oneself upon one's environment. A man is described as possessing moral personality because in the first place he is purposive, and in the second place he can view other men as sharers with him in the good life.

To summarize so far: When Green states that rights are relative to a moral end, he means that they are justified by considerations of the good life which he conceives of in terms of

self-realization. This end is not simply moral conscientiousness, and rights for Green, therefore, are not simply requirements for obedience to a moral law. Moreover, the moral personality or the moral capacity of an individual, in virtue of
which rights and duties can be assigned to him, is a capacity
for purposive activity and self-improvement, not simply an
urge toward greater moral resolution.

In stating what I take to be Green's conception of the end
to which rights are relative, I have not raised and considered
the arguments which have usually been urged against the view
of the *summum bonum* as self-realization. While I think these
arguments are important, my aim has not been to decide
either for or against the theory that the end of man is self-
realization. My purpose has been to show that this is how
Green in fact construes the end. In Green's theory the conception of self-realization is not far from the notion of self-
improvement, and this, according to Green, is a common
enough experience in our lives. (6LP) We do frequently have
the feeling that, consequences apart, we should do better, and
a familiar demand is that things could be better. To realize
the self has something to do with improving the self and one's
situation in life. What is involved in self-improvement cannot
be defined in advance for everybody. While the concept of
self-realization is philosophically obscure, we need not sophis-
ticate ourselves into denying that there is such an experience
as self-improvement and even self-realization.

There is an important element in Green's conception of the
summum bonum which we have not yet examined. Green often
if not always equates "self-realization" with "human perfection." This suggests that not every human capability or interest or need can be admitted as an element in the good life.
For instance, to take Green's favorite example, the capacity
for excessive drinking ought not to be realized. Neither the
drunkard nor those related to him seem to be *better* off when
this capacity has been exercised. There are personal ideals
(such as those of the Mafia) and human capabilities (such as
that of inflicting torture on men and animals) which do not
contribute to the improvement and well-being of *man*. Green
indicates in a general way what he counts as "vicious" self-
realization as opposed to the "virtuous" variety. The man who

"seeks to assert himself, to realize himself, to show what he has in him to be, in achievements which may make the world wonder, but [which] in their social effects are such that the human spirit . . . is not advanced but hindered by them in the realization of its capabilities" is not a sharer in the good life. (176PE) The ends for which he lives require "the depression of others."

The self-realization which each man seeks is an element in the good life and, therefore, a basis for his rights-claims only to the extent that it does not hinder the like pursuits of others. The moral end, then, to which rights are relative is more than just a personal ideal. It is somehow or other an ideal which is or can be common to others besides oneself. Green writes: "To the man living under its influence the idea of the absolutely desirable, the effort to better himself, must from the first express itself in some form of social require-ment. So far as he is set on making his way to some further fulfillment of himself, he must seek to carry those in whom he is interested with him in the process." (202PE) A man's true good, according to Green, is a common good.

It is not easy to determine what Green has in mind when he talks about "a common good." There are many intricate issues involved. But before we try to decide what he means, it might be well to note how he "builds up" his conception of a com-mon good.

According to Green, the individual who pursues various in-terests and ends in an effort to realize himself is a product to a great extent of the society in which he lives and of the man-ifold relationships into which he enters. Moreover, a powerful interest of each individual is that which he has in other per-sons. Green admits that it may "seem unphilosophical nowa-days to accept this distinctive social interest on our part as a primary fact" (200PE), but he doesn't think it cannot be ex-plained. The interests we have in other persons "are not merely interests dependent on other persons for the means to their gratification, but interests *in the good* of those other persons, interests which cannot be satisfied without the consciousness that those other persons are satisfied. The man cannot con-template himself as in a better state, or on the way to the best, without contemplating others, not merely as a means to that better state, but as sharing it with him." (199PE, italics added)

We do not simply wish others well. It seems that the well-being we conceive for ourselves "includes" the well-being of others in some sense. In the pursuit of such well-being there is no opposition between self and others. (235PE) Men are capable of bettering and fulfilling themselves; they conceive of this as an absolute good "in which they include a like bettering or fulfillment of others." (216PE)

It appears to be axiomatic in Green's self-realization ethics that a man's self-regarding interests and his other-regarding interests have equal force. But I am not just interested in others; I actually look upon their "good" as mine and my "good" as theirs. Thus, the moral ideal which up till now we have regarded as self-realization is further characterized by Green as a common good. A man's pursuit of a personal ideal of well-being or self-fulfillment is somehow or other related to a common good.

Only to the extent that individuals recognize a good common to self and others can they justify their rights-claims. As Green sees it, it is not just personal interests and goals which entitle one to rights of all sorts. Only insofar as these are constituent elements in a common good does the individual come to be the possessor of rights. Rights then are justified by the requirements of a common good.

I have not critically analyzed the conception of a common good so far, nor have I tried to show how Green employs it to justify rights. These are important issues which must await further preliminary discussion. While Green believed that the important question is "why rights at all?," it is not the only question he tried to answer. He raises the equally important and perhaps more interesting question of what is required to bring about the *existence* of rights. This question is never explicitly posed; but Green's treatment of the subject of rights in the *Lectures* is, in effect, a discussion of what in the literature has been called the "significance conditions" for rights-talk. It is not that Green analyzes the meaning and use of rights-utterances, but he does outline what he takes to be the necessary conditions which make rights possible.

What we think the existence of rights presupposes probably depends to a large extent on why we think rights are important and what we suppose rights secure or provide. It is likely that considerations relevant to answering the question "why rights at all?" are also pertinent in some way to answering the question "what makes rights possible?" Green's theory exemplifies the relatedness of these questions. Thus, a ground or reason given in support of rights, as we have seen, is that persons ought to be able to realize themselves, i.e., fulfill their desires, achieve their purposes, improve their situation in life, etcetera. But this consideration provides a *condition* for the existence of rights. In order for rights to be, there must be human beings who have desires and interests, who can posit aims and ends for themselves, and who can communicate their demands.

But while these questions are related they are also I think logically distinct. To establish why rights of any kind ought to be acknowledged and allowed is not necessarily to show what is presupposed by the conception of a right. One of the problems with Green's theory is that he does not always divide his discussion along clear lines. We can, however, distinguish two arguments which, while interrelated, can and should be examined separately. One argument in Green's theory has to do with an analysis of conditions, or what has been called the "context" of rights; the other has to do with the justification of rights. In this chapter we have made an overture to the latter argument. It is potentially more fruitful, however, to proceed with our reconstruction of Green's theory by examining the former argument. When we have understood what the conditions are, we will be in a better position to determine, first, what Green meant by "a common good"; second, how this is for him a principle according to which we can determine rights; and third, how rights contribute to or constitute a common good.

CHAPTER 4

Persons and Society

If there are going to be any rights at all, there have to be persons, for they are the exemplary subjects of rights. This is a very obvious point and no theory of rights need insist on it. But there is a sense in which the statement is not, at least, trivially true. When Green insists that only among persons in the moral or ethical sense of "person" can there come to be rights, he is recommending a specific sense of the term. On this sense it is not trivially true that rights inhere in persons. Indeed, one may decide that it is not true at all.[1]

We have noted that in Green's theory the possession of moral personality is an important condition for rights. But the notion of moral personality must be scrutinized further. In the previous chapter we examined one aspect of Green's conception of the end to which rights are relative. Consistent with the reading of the ultimate end as self-realization and well-being, it was suggested that the "moral capacity" is a capacity for purposive activity and for desiring and pursuing a personal ideal which is not simply an ideal of the virtuous will. It was suggested further that it is a capacity for the good life. For Green, "moral person" means the human being who has desires and ideals and is capable of pursuing goals. He writes: "Every right implies a person as its subject but in the moral sense, since all rights depend on that capacity in the individual for being determined by a conception of well-being, as an object at once for himself and for others which constitutes personality in the moral sense." (150LP) "Moral" here has the force of "purposive." To be determined by a conception of well-being is to posit and to try to achieve such an end. The term "moral" has another meaning as well, but let us postpone comment on this for the moment.

The moral personality, however, is further characterized by Green as a "rational will." (27LP) Whatever else Green means by this, there is evidence in the *Lectures* that by "rational will" he understands "practical reason," which he identifies as the "capacity in a man of conceiving the perfection of his nature as an object to be attained by action." (6LP) Again, we are not concerned now about the perfection of self which is a particular conceptualized goal. We are more interested in the fact that rational will, or practical reason, has to do with the ability to conceptualize (imagine, project) a desired end and to act consciously with some "reasoned-out" program to achieve this end. Green seems to be saying that only persons possessing an ability to conceptualize goals and to act on "syllogistic reasoning," as it were, come to have rights.

Now, does he mean that persons possess rights *in virtue of* this ability? If he does, then it would appear that those who lack practical reason, either because it is not a capacity in them or because it has been impaired—e.g., infants, lunatics, idiots, the senile—do not have rights. Yet Green does not hesitate to affirm that such creatures have a right to life. (154LP) Rights, or at least the right to life, is attributed to the human embryo, the idiot, and the lunatic on the basis of other considerations. It must be admitted that Green's attempts to locate these relevant considerations are somewhat torturous. For instance, the lunatic has a right to life not because he has reason but because, one, he may "in another life" and under "unearthly" conditions exhibit the required capacity, or two, he serves a social purpose by being the object of "affectionate ministrations." (154LP) The fact that Green does "cast about" for other characteristics of the human situation on whose basis rights can be ascribed, however strained the casting, seems to indicate that he did not wish to maintain that human beings have rights in virtue of their capacity to reason practically. It is true that he attaches great importance to this capacity, but he does say that the right to life belongs to man "in virtue simply of his human nature." (155LP) And human nature includes a host of attributes and characteristics.

What Green wants to maintain with respect to the possession of rational will as a condition for rights is this: there must be some form of reasoned activity consequent upon conceptualized purposes in order for there to be rights. Put another way, there must be some persons who conceive of ends which they proceed to achieve by means of intelligent action. The possibility of rights does not require that *every* subject of rights possess a rational will or practical reason.

Green is not being inconsistent here. In allowing rights to the mentally indigent and to the generally incapable he is not threatening his fundamental thesis that rights are related to the conscious pursuit of ends and goals. He is simply saying that in order to get the conception of a right formulated in the first place there has to be some sort of consciously purposive activity. Someone has to be aware that he has a life to call his own and that he wants to realize this life in some way. Green, of course, would have to say that in a universe consisting solely of lunatics, idiots, and infants, i.e., beings who are not conscious of themselves, there would be no rights.

But, further, and what for Green appears to be a corollary of the possession of rational will, the moral personality is a "capacity on the part of the individual for making a common good his own." (26LP) Being moral, then, is being aware that others also pursue ends and that these ends are related in some way to one's own. According to Green, one can have rights only as a member of a community or society whose members recognize a common good "as their own ideal good, as that which should be for each of them." (25LP) The existence of rights presupposes a community in which an ideal of some kind (a common good) is conceptually acknowledged.

Now, it is not immediately clear what is required for rights "to begin." Let us assume for now that the capacity for making a common good one's own is a capacity, among other things, for membership in a community. What exactly, then, do rights presuppose? It appears that they require *both* the capacity for communal membership as well as the actual community. A person possesses the power to make a common good his own, and this makes rights possible. But it is only in the community that this capacity is evinced and it is only as a member of the community that he can claim the right to exercise this power as well as others. The community, therefore, is a necessary condition for the existence of rights. No rights can exist apart from it.

The discussion has taken a somewhat paradoxical turn. But in this apparent paradox lies an important thesis of Green's theory of rights. While I will have to return to this point in a later chapter, I set it down now somewhat cryptically and perhaps dogmatically. The point is this: It seems that for Green rights, specifically, "natural" or human rights, are a condition for the realization and development of community. Community is possible when a common good, whatever this is, becomes a personal ideal. The good life for Green is possible only in a certain form of community, and rights contribute to the achievement of such a community. The apparent paradox arises from Green's insistence that rights can only exist within the framework of a community or society. There must be some sort of community before rights can begin. Now, either there is a community or we need rights to create one. But it is possible that for Green this is not a case of "either-or." The community in one sense of the term is a condition for rights and in another sense is the result of rights.

To return. What has been said so far is that a condition for the existence of rights is the existence of persons who have desires, who are capable of consciously purposive activity, and who further are capable of making a common good their own. This capacity presupposes membership in a community. So we must say that another condition for the existence of rights is some sort of community.

What is a community or society for Green? In what way is the community a condition for rights? What does Green mean when he argues that rights cannot exist apart from a community or society? Before attempting to answer these questions, it is important to examine briefly some aspects of Green's criticism of the classical doctrine of natural rights. It should be noted that the accuracy of Green's reading of this theory is not an issue here. What is of interest are the objections he has to the theory. By noting these we obtain a clue as to why he thought that rights could not exist anterior to or independently of a community or society.

The first point to notice, which has apparently escaped one critic and possibly another, is that Green does not object to the use of the term "natural" in the phrase "natural rights" where this means fundamental and independent of enacted law. According to H. A. Prichard, Green denies "that you or I who are members of a state have any moral rights or obligations apart from a law (i.e., a ruler's action of ordering and enforcing the acts in question)."[2] Green denies nothing of the sort, as we will note. When he objects to the conception of rights involved in the classical doctrine it is not because he reserves the term "rights" for legal rights only. What Green clearly implies in his theory is that rights are related to certain moral rules and principles and, further, that they depend on the enforcement, in some sense, of these rules. He writes, "The general fabric of rights in any society does not depend on the existence of a definite and ascertained sovereignty in the restricted sense of the words . . . but on the control of the conduct of men according to certain regular principles by a society recognizing common interests." (103LP) Rights cannot be divorced from rules and principles. This does not mean that they are not independent of a government's order.

The subject of Green's inquiry in the *Lectures* is not the entire realm of rights but primarily those rights which "are antecedent to the state [and] which are not derived from it but may exist where a state is not." (247LP) Unlike legal rights these rights have not become the subject of coercive legal rules. But like legal rights they are related to certain rules, and, further, they *can* be enforced by law though they do not cease to be rights even when not legally protected. (8LP)

The distinction Green makes between moral duties and obligations reveals what he has in mind when he implies that rights of all sorts admit of some sort of enforcement. The obligations correlative to rights are to be distinguished from moral duties: "When obligations then are spoken of in this connection as . . . correlative to rights, they must always be understood not as moral duties, not as relative to states of will, but as relative to outward acts, of which the performance or omission can and should be enforced." (10LP) Moral duties proper are duties to act from certain motives and dispositions, and the latter cannot be enforced.

The possessor of a right can insist on the performance of the correlative obligation, for the latter can be enforced.[3] In this sense rights admit of enforcement and, further, can be incorporated into a legal system. But though not all rights are enforced by law it does not follow that they are not valid. There is a "true and important sense in which natural rights and obligations exist," writes Green. This is the sense in which, according to Aristotle, the state is natural; that is, only insofar as they are necessary for the fulfillment of a "moral capacity without which a man would not be a man." (30LP)

Green's objection, then, to the conception of rights in the classical doctrine does not arise from his belief that all rights are the arbitrary creations of law. He does not believe this; he expressly denies it. What he does object to is the idea implicit in the theory that there are rights which men possess independently of society, that these rights were brought with them into a society which they contracted to form.

Green realizes that the "contract" is a historical fiction. He is not opposed to the use of a fiction, such as the state of nature, to convey a true conception of some moral relation of man. (49LP) The objection to such a fiction is that it conveys "a false notion of rights." Green's criticism of Hobbes and Locke turns upon the issue of whether the "state of nature" implies society in any sense of the term. The writers are not clear on this matter. If it was a state of *bellum omnium contra omnes,* then the contract is impossible. (47LP) If, on the other hand, as Locke implies, it was a state governed by a law of nature where men observe obligations to each other and admit rights without a legal imponent but just the consciousness and reason of man, then such a state is already "in principle" a political society and a contract is not required to form it. (54LP) It should be noted parenthetically here that Green's use of the phrase "in principle" covers a multitude of sins, but this affects his theory about what constitutes a political society. For Green, apparently, the idea of a *contract* to form a viable society is a logically impossible one. Men either are or they are not "in society." In either case a contract is impossible, or rather, it makes no sense. A corollary of this is that a right existing in a state of nature which is not a state of society is a contradiction. (31LP)

The target of Green's criticism against the contract theorists is their apparent belief that rights can be held independent of operative social rules and one's membership in a society.[4] According to Green, all rights are held in relation to a community or society where there are rules that define the rights. But Green is not merely saying that rights imply social relations between human beings. In insisting on the community as a condition for the existence of rights he is saying that a man *becomes* the possessor of rights only as a member of a community or society where the members stand in some special relation to each other.

In what sense does a man *become* the possessor of rights as a member of a society or community? We will examine this question first and then consider the sort of relations which, according to Green, must characterize the community or society upon which rights depends. The aim of the discussion which follows is to try to understand what Green meant when he argued that rights *depend* on a community or society. This theme is pursued in later chapters as well.

According to Green, a human being becomes a *person* only in society. To be a person, as we have seen, is to be purposive, to act consciously and intelligently to achieve goals which have to do with one's well-being. Personality in this sense is actualized in society: "Only through society is anyone enabled to give that effect to the idea of himself as the object of his actions, to the idea of a possible better state of himself, without which the idea would remain like that of space to a man who had not the senses either of sight or touch." (190PE)

Personality is developed when a man "gives effect" to a conceptualized ideal. I suppose Green means here that only when one actually *acts* to achieve an ideal, in this case, a better state of himself, does he become a person, i.e., a subject of rights. The mere "intellectual entertaining" of an ideal or an end is not enough to make one a subject of rights. And it is only in society that one can act consciously to realize an ideal. Why is this so? Because, according to Green, an essential condition for becoming conscious of, and realizing, a personal ideal, is "some practical recognition of . . . an 'I' by a 'Thou' and a 'Thou' by an 'I.' " (190PE)

This is all highly obscure. It is not clear how this "practical recognition" enables me to consciously pursue an ideal. For the moment, and despite the obscurity, we could say that

Green's point is probably more familiar than it is profound. He seems to be saying that we become persons in the moral sense when we regard ourselves as such and we "learn to regard ourselves as persons among other persons because we are treated as such." (190PE) To treat another as a person is to treat him as entitled to have a will of his own and as being an end in himself.

Perhaps what this amounts to in the final analysis is the proposition that it is only within society that men can develop into rational and moral beings. This is an idea with which many would concur, though we may not agree about what it is that society provides which makes a man rational and moral nor do we always know what it means to *be* rational and moral. For Green, apparently, society provides that regular and intimate contact with others which we require to build up an image of self as having a place or "a station with its duties." When Green writes that only through the action of society does the individual come "practically to conceive his personality," he means that only in relating to and communicating with others do we come to know who we are and what we are about. Moreover, when he talks about the role of society in developing personality, he employs "society" in its widest sense to include any intimate grouping of people, for example, the family, which is an early and basic form of society or community.

But, further, only in society do we develop our so-called higher qualities and the interests we have in bringing about a better life for ourselves and others—"society supplies all the higher content to this conception." (190PE) If, then, human beings become rational and moral creatures only by living in a society, and rights can exist only among rational and moral persons, it is clear that only by living in a society can a man become the possessor of rights.

Some remarks are in order. How a man becomes a moral and rational being capable of acknowledging rights and obligations is a deep question. It doesn't seem that the philosopher is in any privileged position with respect to any answers. In fact, he may be less qualified than other students of human nature to provide an answer. Green's analysis of the relationship between society and the development of personality is less than adequate but it is not clear what would count as an *adequate* analysis. If in the quoted passages about the "actualization" of personality Green intends to assert *more* than the belief that the individual acquires moral and rational attributes in the process of interacting with others, then his thesis is not altogether cogent. What needs to be indicated here, however, is that his view of the formation of personality does not commit him to the thesis that society is *axiologically* prior to the individual.

This thesis has been imputed to the Idealists in general, but it is not substantiated in Green's case. There is a powerful individualism in Green's moral and social philosophy deriving from his firm belief in the "ultimate worth" of the individual person. As W. D. Lamont has written, "To Green, more than any other member of the Idealist school, belongs the honour of having kept in the forefront of ethics the conception of the individual person as an end-in-himself."[5] It is important to bear this in mind when we consider his contention that rights inhere in individuals only as members of a society or community.

Most proponents of a form of natural rights theory have emphasized that certain rights are had by men *qua* men, "and not only if they are members of some society or stand in some special relation to each other."[6] It is admitted, however, even by those who advance such a thesis, that a belief in the individual rights of man is not incompatible with the view that the individual has rights and duties only in the presence of others.[7] In other words, to say that one has rights as a man is not to imply that these rights can exist apart from a society or social grouping of some kind.

Green does not deny that men have rights *qua* men provided we understand by "man" a creature who is capable of living and relating with others in some way. What Green denies is that "being-a-man" is radically different in meaning from "being-a-member-of-a-society." The concept of a human being employed by the philosopher who is concerned about rights is different from that employed by a biologist or physiologist. When we say that rights inhere in human beings, we mean by "human being" someone who is actually or potentially a social and moral being. As A. I. Melden has pointed out, "we can say of the term 'human being' that it is a forensic term that applies to beings who are morally concerned and morally accountable."[8] This is precisely Green's point. Man is the subject of rights, but a man who is among men and who is in some sense morally concerned and morally accountable. On the other hand, it does not seem likely that John Locke would have denied this.

Of course, the thrust of all natural rights theories is their insistence that certain rights of the individual are fundamental and may not be denied, because they are the "fundamental conditions of *human* social life and government."[9] But Green too holds that certain rights are fundamental. He writes, "The essential thing in political society is a power which guarantees men's rights" and, further, "the political society is more complete as the freedom guaranteed is more complete, both in respect of the persons enjoying it and of the range of possible actions and acquisitions over which it extends." (91LP) The important point to note here—the issue on which Green diverges from other Idealists and especially from D. Ritchie, with whose doctrine his own is often confused—is this: While Green maintains that a man becomes the possessor of rights only in a society and that therefore society is a condition for rights, he is not saying that rights are determined only by the needs and conveniences of society as a whole. Green does say that rights are related in some sense to a common good, but that is a wholly different matter. Before we go into that, some more things need to be said about society as a condition for rights.

What sort of relations constitute a community or society for Green? Are they casual and intermittent? Does "society" mean more than just a mere contact between rational and irrational creatures? If rights cannot be held independent of society, what exactly is this "dependence?"

According to Green, society is founded upon the "practical recognition" and interest of persons in each other. Without this recognition and interest there would be nothing to countervail the selfish, egoistical tendencies which are natural to man. It is this interest which makes the "combination of men . . . for common ends" possible. (190PE) The characteristic mark of this social interest is that "to the man who is the subject of it, those who are its objects are ends, in the same sense in which he is an end to himself . . . they are included in the end for which he lives in living for himself." (200PE) Green takes it to be an "ultimate fact of human history" that "out of sympathies of animal origin, through their presence in a self-conscious soul, there arise interests as of a person in a person." (201PE) And every community is founded on such self-conscious interests.

What is interesting here is that a community or society is described as a combination of men pursuing common ends. The relations which exist between individuals in a community are not wholly casual. They are "relations dear and all the charities of father, son, and brother." (201PE) Green, however, does not elaborate on or analyze these relations. He is content to say merely that every society even in its narrowest and most primitive forms rests on the "treatment by one human being of another as an end." (190PE) In the *Lectures* he insists on the peculiarly intimate character of social relationships. A man and his rights depend on society in a way in which "the gravity of a body depends on relations to other bodies" (99LP) and thought depends on language. (114LP)

Now it may be that the well-being and progress of a society depend on the mutual respect and interest of which Green speaks. But, again, what makes society possible in the first place is a large question. It is not clear that it is a function solely of the interests Green talks about. His conception of what constitutes a society appears to limit the term to what some writers have called "elective societies," groups of people, that is, who come together for the sake of pursuing some common interest.[10] There are problems involved in such a view, especially if it is society in *this* sense that is a condition for the existence of rights. But I do not think Green means to say that rights depend on the total congruence of individual interests and purposes. He does imply that a society in which persons do have a conception of rights is one where the "moral point of view" is predominant. In this sense there are, for Green, certain relations which must obtain between persons if we are to say of them that they form a society where rights are acknowledged.

What are these relations? Obviously, for Green, the existence of any number of persons within a certain territory who never communicate with each other either by means of language or gesture, who just pass each other by, would not constitute a society. Physical contiguity is not enough. Some communication and other sorts of transactions must characterize the relations between persons. Society is indicated by reference to the transactions that occur as well as the mutual expectations which underlie these transactions. But in order for there to be either expectations or transactions there must be certain favorable dispositions which function to sustain the former.

We might explain Green's position by means of the following consideration: There are at least two ways in which one can be said to *belong* to a particular organization such as, for example, The Society for the Preservation of Historical Monuments in ——. First, one belongs, i.e., is a member insofar as one pays one's dues or signs a form indicating interest in the aims of the society; second, one belongs in the sense that one participates actively in the meetings of the society and undertakes to do various tasks for the achievement of the aims of the society. He who simply pays his dues and never attends a meeting does not enter into appropriate relations with other members nor does he have the "right attitude." The participator, on the other hand, has the needed attitude and cooperates with the others.

The example indicates what for Green must characterize the relations which constitute a society or community upon which rights depend. Those who compose such a society are not mere "dues payers" who may or may not come into contact with each other. They are "participators" in the sense that they meet together to communicate and to transact business.

There are, however, important differences between the particular organization in our example and a more general community where persons are grouped. To return to Green's language, it is not the case that all the members of such a community must have *consciously* before their minds the well-being of each other or the achievement of a unitary goal. In an ordinary community there are no weekly meetings to attend nor is one always thinking about a unitary goal. The relations and reactions that characterize the ordinary community are

"habitual and instinctive." (121LP) The attitude, however is
the right one. The members of a community in which rights
can be conceived have the moral point of view and their relations reflect this attitude.

To summarize briefly: I have tried to clarify and explain
what Green means when he argues that rights *depend* on society. Thus far we have noted two possible senses of "depend."
First, rights depend on society in the sense that the moral personality is formed or developed in a community or society,
and only among persons who are rational and moral to some
degree can there come to be rights. Second, rights depend on
society in the sense that they presuppose some interested contact between human beings, a contact characterized by the
moral point of view.

Some further remarks are in order. Rights do not come to
be among rational and moral beings just because they can
acknowledge that duties and rights can be held against them.
The correlativity of rights and duties is accepted by Green,
but it is not analyzed nor made the fundamental fact about
rights. Some have argued that Man Friday has rights because
Robinson Crusoe is capable of having duties. Indeed, in the
words of one writer, this "constituted a superiority on the
European's part and was one of the earlier instances of the
white man's burden."[11] Green would say that Friday has rights
but not primarily because Robinson Crusoe has duties to him.
Both men have rights because they have interests and ends in
common and each is as much a person as the other. According to Green, Crusoe could not be considered morally
superior to Friday. Their moral worth is the same and their
rights depend on this.

Again, the interested contact which characterizes the community upon which rights depend need not be "regular and
intimate" all the time.[12] Green would say that the possessor of
rights must have had some intimate contact with some human
beings at some point in his life. Thus, even though Friday and
Robinson Crusoe do not have what might be considered regular and intimate contact at the outset, there are rights between
them because each man has been a member of a community
where such contact was available to him.

The two senses of "depend" examined so far pose no conceptual difficulties, though we may not in fact agree with either the conception of personality or that of society presented in Green's theory. There is, however, a third sense in which he maintains that rights depend on society, and here there are conceptual difficulties. In the *Prolegomena* and especially in the *Lectures* Green insists that rights require social recognition. In the sense that rights are "made" by recognition, they depend for their existence on a community or society.

What Green means by "recognition" and how this is a condition for rights are issues examined in the following chapter.

CHAPTER 5

Rights, Claims, and Recognition

It is Green's idea that rights cannot exist apart from a community or society because, among other considerations, all rights require recognition. This central thesis in his theory is unfortunately never adequately analyzed by Green himself. Critical reviews of the idea that rights are made by recognition range from regarding it either as an "absurd phrase" or as totally irrelevant to the conception of moral and human rights.[1] Since social recognition is an extremely vague concept anyway, it is further tempting in Green's case to offer peculiar readings of this idea which make one wonder how anyone could attach importance to such a notion. It will not be my contention that the views of Green are immune to criticism; but they deserve to be more carefully stated. Further, the doctrine that rights are made by recognition ought to be seriously considered for the light it may throw on the issue of what it means for rights to exist or for someone to have a right.

In the literature, the concept of a right has been explicated mainly in terms of the concept of duty. But writers have also noted that a description of the various kinds of duties that are correlated with rights is not enough to elucidate the concept of a right. Some analysis of claims and claiming appears to be needed for an understanding of what rights are.[2] To this growing context of the subject of rights the idea that claims require recognition in some sense should be added and analyzed. The manner in which claims are asserted and acknowledged involves recognition, and the extent to which a claim is recognized determines the extent to which a right exists in a significant sense—i.e., as a real right and not merely as a paper right. I hope to make this last statement clearer while I examine Green's doctrine that rights are made by recognition.

It has been maintained that the idea that rights are made or created by recognition is equivalent to a certain metaethical view about the nature of rights.[3] We must realize at the outset that *Green's* notion is not intended to be a view about how rights are known or how rights-statements may be analyzed. Nor is he saying that statements in which "recognize" occurs function primarily ascriptively and not descriptively. He might, if he had thought about it, have assented to such a view.[4] His theory, however, is not a theory about the logic of rights-discourse. If we had to classify his view, we would say that it was a more or less sociological account (a philosophically oriented sociology to be sure) of how rights come to be. Thus, Green might be puzzled by the assertion that rights may exist in a normative though not in a metaethical sense, and that while a reversal of social recognition would very probably destroy a right, this is destruction in the metaethical not in the normative sense. As far as Green is concerned, where there is no recognition there are no rights in any sense.

In the *Lectures* Green defines a right variously. It will be necessary to use a number of quotations in order to show that a group of notions is involved in Green's conception of a right as well as in that of recognition. A right, we are told, is "a power claimed and recognized as contributory to a common good." (99LP) Again, a right is "a power of which the exercise by the individual or by some body of men is recognized by a society ... as itself directly essential to a common good." (103LP) Further on we read: "A right is a power of acting for his own ends—for what he conceives to be his good—secured to an individual by the community." (208LP) Rights can exist only "in a society of men recognising each other as *isoi kai omoioi.* They are constituted by that mutual recognition." (139LP)

Very early in the *Lectures* Green introduces the notion of recognition, and throughout the text, merely through the force of repetition alone, we become aware of the importance he attached to it. The "recognition of a power," he writes, *"in some way or other,* as that which should be, is always necessary to render it a right." (23LP, italics added) Again, "there can be no right without a consciousness of common interest on the part of members of a society. Without this there might be certain powers on the part of individuals, but no *recognition* of these powers by others as powers of which they allow the exercise, nor any *claim* to such recognition; and without this recognition or claim to recognition there can be no right." (31LP, italics added)

Several issues can be distinguished in these quoted statements. Green rightly or wrongly takes what he calls the "common" or "public interest" or the "common good" as being some sort of grounds for the claiming and justification of rights. When he says that there can be no rights without a consciousness of common interest or a recognition of a common good, he means that rights are justified by considerations of a common good. But it is not clear that the recognition of a power which actually renders it a right is the same thing as the recognition of a common good. Nor is it certain that the recognition by men of each other as *isoi kai omoioi*, which constitutes rights, is the same as the recognition of common interests.

We have already noted in chapter three above that there are two arguments in Green's theory which, while related, can be examined separately. One is an analysis of conditions, the other has to do with justification. Green's idea that rights are made by recognition in some sense is part of his analysis of those conditions which must obtain for rights to exist. They provide an answer to the question: how are rights possible? The common good, on the other hand, justifies rights. It answers the question: why rights at all?

Critics of Green have invariably confused the recognition of a power or a claim with the recognition of a common good. It has been supposed that the recognition which makes rights is equivalent to an awareness or consciousness or an opinion. As against this interpretation I propose the following: The term "recognition" as Green employs it is not univocal. Green uses it in at least two senses and possibly a third; these are implicit in his theory. There is first of all recognition (a) in the sense of certain appropriate action or response; this action ensures that a right may be exercised or enjoyed. The other sense of recognition (b) is that of "consciousness" of a common good; such a consciousness or awareness provides the principle according to which the recognition (a) of a claim is justified.

The third sense of recognition is that of respect, and this is the sense involved when Green speaks of the recognition by men of each other, as *isoi kai omoioi.*

All three "kinds" of recognition are important for the existence of rights but they do not achieve the same thing. The "making" of a right for Green is an extremely complicated affair. The discussion which follows is an attempt to map out Green's argument. First, I shall discuss the different senses of "recognition" as well as the meaning of the oft-quoted phrase "there is no right 'but thinking makes it so.'" (136LP) Next, I shall discuss the "objects" of the recognition which makes rights. Here attention is focused on claims, claiming, and equality. The following section deals with the source of recognition, the question, that is, of *who* recognizes. Finally, I shall consider why Green attached such importance to recognition as a condition for rights. I shall try to determine where in the format of rights recognition enters, that is, whether it is a condition for the having or the exercising of rights. Green does not clearly indicate what he means by "made by" in the phrase "rights are made by recognition." The question is: what, for Green, is it to *make* a right? Is it to *claim, assert, have, exercise, enjoy* a right, or what? We must try to answer this question before we can decide why recognition is important for rights.

Those who admit that legal rights are related to recognition (though what it means for a law to "recognize" a right is not always clear; for example, does a law "create" a right or does it protect an existing moral right when it recognizes it, etcetera) are not willing to grant that moral and human rights depend on recognition. Thus, A. C. Ewing writes: "Obviously a legal right depends on recognition by some constituted authority or by the legal code itself; but it does not follow that a moral right does so and . . . it is surely out of the question to suppose that recognition by anybody could constitute a moral right or that non-recognition of his moral rights could deprive an individual of them."[5] Even if we grant that the rights of an individual depend on the social good likely to be secured by his having the rights, this does not mean, according to Ewing, that rights depend on recognition. Green's idea seems to derive from "a desire to find a middle term between legal and moral rights." This desire has produced a confusion in Green's thinking.[6] W. D. Ross presents a view similar to that expressed by Ewing. According to Ross, Green takes recognition to be the common denominator between legal and moral rights. In the former case, recognition consists in the making of a law; in the latter, it consists simply in public opinion. Green is wrong on both counts. The details of Ross's position need not detain us here. His point is that Green mistakenly makes a moral right "depend not on the nature of a given person and his relations to his fellows, but on what people think about them, i.e., on what a majority of the community think about them."[7] Ross's criticism has been reiterated by many others.

The assumption that underlies all these observations—we can scarcely call them "arguments"—is that recognition is equivalent to public opinion and this opinion creates rights. This assumption does less than justice to Green's view. As for his desire to find a common denominator between different types of rights, this is to his credit. While there are differences between legal and moral rights, there are also great similarities, and the study of the former can tell us a great deal about the nature of other kinds of rights.

Green nowhere equates recognition with mere opinion. To suppose that he did is to reduce his thesis to a point which scarcely merits attention. Moreover, while Green does argue that "thinking" has something to do with rights, he does not deny that they depend on the nature of persons and their relations with each other. This should be clear from the discussion in the previous chapter.

"Recognition" is a complex term. If we attend carefully to the various contexts in which it occurs in Green's writing, we will note that he employs it in different senses depending on what is recognized and what this recognition brings about. Thus, the recognition of powers and claims "regulates" in some way. When powers are so regulated, rights exist. A man's "moral personality," Green writes, "is developed through rights, i.e., through the recognition by members of a society of powers in each other contributory to a common good, and the regulation of these powers by that recognition." (26LP) Again, recognition is "rational" and as such it is the source of morality, for it is only "as recognizing common interests and objects, that individuals come to have these [moral] attributes and rights." (113LP) On the other hand, individuals, according to Green, "habitually and instinctively" regard their claims as mutual. (121LP) A man's claim "is conditional upon his recognising a like claim in others." (121LP) The suggestion here is that this recognizing, whatever it is, is habitual and instinctive. But claims are "constituted" by the consciousness of a certain end to which a person may direct his powers and capacities and the "recognition of them by a society as capable of such direction . . . renders them actually rights." (41LP) In this context Green adds, "it is only thinking that makes a might a right." (41LP)

It has been necessary to quote several passages in order to illustrate the point to be argued for, namely, that Green does not appear to use the term "recognition" in the same sense throughout his discussion. Let us begin, however, by considering one of Green's most often quoted statements, namely, "There is no right 'but thinking makes it so.' " (136LP) Much philosophical abuse has been directed at Green on account of this sentence. No one seems to have noticed that the crucial words are in quotation marks, Green's own. In the context in which they occur he explains what he means by them, thus hinting perhaps that we are not to take them literally. Several critics, however, have taken them quite literally. John Plamenatz, for one, accuses Green of arguing like the subjectivists who believed that the *esse* of objects is *percipi*. In saying that rights are made by thought, Plamenatz charges that Green "confuses knowing and making."[8]

But it is not Green who is confused, for he does not mean that my thinking that I have a right or anyone else's thinking the same thing is sufficient to create or secure that right for me. In the context from which this statement is drawn, as well as in other sections where thinking is linked to rights, Green makes his meaning plain. The concept of a right, like the concepts of duty and obligation, derives from the ways in which men view themselves, their purposes, and each other. A right is real, but it is not to be reduced simply to a power producing sensible effects. (38LP) It is related to an insensible function in the individual, that being the power to conceive of cer-

tain ends or that which is good. I do not have a right simply
because I *can* do this or that. For I *can* do many things which
I would not ordinarily claim *a right* to do. According to Green,
I have a right to do that which is good for me to do. But this
"good" is something which I and perhaps others conceive or
imagine or think about. In this sense a right "derives" from a
conception.

When Green says a right is an "ideal attribute," he does not
mean that there is no empirical evidence which would count
toward confirming the sentence "X has a right R." He does
imply that the meaning of "a right" is not fully explicated
merely by pointing to such evidence. We require an idea or
principle which itself is not verifiable, at least not sensibly.
When we establish that rights exist in a given society, the
rights themselves are not sensibly verified. A number of other
things are verified, which indicate whether or not individuals
are enjoying or exercising their rights. Rights do not exist in
the minds of men, though the way men think, i.e., imagine,
entertain, or project ideals and purposes, has much to do with
what rights they will admit and recognize.

The point to be made here is that thought, in Green's
theory, is related to that insensible side of rights which has to
do with their "ground" or justification. This is what Green intends when he says "only thinking makes a might a right." If I
can justify the exercise of my power in terms of an acceptable
ideal I can *claim* a right. But I have not thereby "made" or
secured a right for myself. It is recognition that secures rights,
i.e., converts claims and powers to rights, and recognition
does not simply mean thinking. Plamenatz assumes that Green
always equates recognition with thinking. In doing so he has
missed a fundamental point in Green's theory.

Green uses "recognition" in at least two senses, the sense of
acknowledgment accompanied by some appropriate action,
and the sense of cognizance or realization, where appropriate
action is not necessarily forthcoming. Ordinary language sanctions both uses. Let us consider some instances where the
term might be used. Suppose I accuse X of spreading vicious
rumors about me and then discover that Y is the culprit. I say,
"I recognize my mistake." What I am doing is acknowledging
or admitting my mistake *and* offering my apologies to X. But

consider the following instance: I have been told repeatedly that if I do not put my barbecue set indoors after using it, it will rust. I do not do so and one day discover that the basin is not fit for use. I say, "I recognize that I should have put it indoors." What I am "doing" here is realizing something though not necessarily acting on my realization. As a matter of fact, while I recognize, i.e., know now, that I should have put the set indoors, my new set has been outdoors since the moment I purchased it.

The difference between the two cases is, first of all, in the "objects" that are recognized, and second, in what the "act" of recognition consists. In the first case I recognize that I have falsely accused someone; in the second, I recognize an ordinary natural fact. When I recognize that I have falsely accused someone, I act in a certain way—I apologize or make amends. The meaning of "recognize" here implies some appropriate action. On the other hand, I need not act at all when I recognize a natural fact, and yet it can still be said that I recognize it. It may be urged that, in both cases, what I recognize "ultimately" is a principle or rule of some kind. This may be granted. The point still remains, however, that recognition in the first case implies action of some kind whereas it does not in the second instance.

Green employs both of these senses of "recognition" in his theory. When he says that we recognize the power or claim of someone to some action, he means that we acknowledge and concede this claim, we respond and act accordingly. This response renders the power of action into a right of action. In discussing the rights of the slave, Green writes that the ordinary citizens who recognize the claims of the slave respond to the latter as a man and a brother and that "this response supplies the factor of social recognition which, as we have seen, is necessary in order to render the exercise of any power a right." (144LP) In the lecture on property rights Green refers to the "recognition by others of a man's appropriations as something which they will treat as not theirs, and the *guarantee* to him of his appropriations by means of that recognition." (211LP, italics added) The recognition, then, which creates rights is viewed as a response and a guarantee. In both cases action of some sort is implied.

When, however, Green says that in a given society individuals recognize a common good, he means that they are aware that their own interests and purposes coincide with those of their fellows. No response or action follows necessarily upon such awareness. Green argues in both the *Prolegomena* and the *Lectures* that neither the awareness of a common good nor the possession of rights means that the individual actively makes a common good his own.

The immediate object of recognition (a) is a claim; that of recognition (b) is a common good. What I am maintaining is that, for Green, it is not the recognition of a common good which "makes" rights. It is the response in the face of a claim which is demanded that "makes" rights. The distinction that is implicit in Green's theory is between recognition in the sense of response or appropriate action, and recognition in the sense of consciousness or intellectual realization. Recognition in the first sense functions to secure rights; recognition in the second sense provides a justification of the response or action that renders mere powers into rights. When I recognize another's claim, I allow its exercise and act in any number of ways to ensure the right. I justify such action, according to Green, by my recognition of the fact that the exercise of this right is contributory to a common good. This is the *ground* for my recognition of the claim.

The fact that most critics have interpreted the notion of recognition solely in terms of consciousness or thinking suggests that Green's view has been confused with that of a disciple. In the literature Green's ideas have frequently been filtered through the views of philosophers on whom he exerted an influence. This has been done on the pretext that these others have written more clearly and less ambiguously than Green. Whether or not this is true, I am inclined to agree with L. T. Hobhouse, who wrote that in Green "we get most of the cream of Idealism and least of its sour milk."[9]

On the issue of recognition it was actually Bernard Bosanquet who maintained that recognition is a mental attitude of sorts. He wrote, "We are said to 'recognize' anything when it comes to us with a consciousness of familiarity." Further on we read, "If my mind has *no* attitude to yours, there is no interdependence and I cannot be party to securing you rights. . . . If my mind *has* an attitude of yours, then there is certainly a recognition between us," and presumably I can be a party to securing you rights.[10] Bosanquet leaves it open as to whether recognition is merely a "mental encounter" when he writes that "the nature of that recognition and what it involves are matters for reasoning and appeal to experience."[11] But as far as I can make out, all Bosanquet is saying is that when I recognize anything, be it person, fact, rule, etcetera, I have an attitude toward it. If, then, I recognize your claim, I have an attitude toward it, and this secures your claim as a right. Now it does not follow from my having an attitude to a person that I will concede his claim on demand. I may have a negative attitude or an indifferent one. This may not be a fair objection because Bosanquet might mean by "recognition" a "right" or positive attitude, the kind, furthermore, that is active. But he provides no hint that this is what he means, and I think it is fair to say that his view of recognition more easily lends itself to the interpretation which has been forced upon Green's view and which has been argued against in this section.

Perhaps a brief summary is in order. There is in Green's theory an implicit distinction between the recognition of a claim or power and the recognition of common interests or a common good. The factor of social recognition which, according to Green, renders a power of action into a right of action is not a mental attitude, such as an opinion or intellectual realization. To recognize a power or a claim is *to act* or behave in ways appropriate to the contents of the demand. To recognize a common good, on the other hand, is *to realize* or be aware that one shares ends, interests, or ideals with others. The intellectual realization of social well-being, or whatever it is "a common good" refers to, provides a ground or justification for the recognition of claims. Though how this is done, how, that is, the *realization* of *a common good* secures rights, has not been discussed so far.

Some have argued that, on epistemological grounds, recognition cannot be a condition for rights. Something has to exist first in order to be recognized. Green is said to have committed a patent epistemological error when he makes the existence of a right depend on its being recognized in order to exist. W. D. Ross writes, "To recognize a thing . . . is to recognize it as existing already."[12] But, and Ross quickly realizes this, Green does not make the existence of a right depend on the recognition of *it*. It is not rights that are recognized, but claims and powers. Green has not violated the doctrine that a thing must exist in order to be recognized.

We have already noted that recognition is *of* many things—powers, claims, equality *(isoi kai omoioi)*, a common good. Now let us consider, first, what sorts of claims are rights-claims, according to Green, and therefore the objects, properly speaking, of the recognition which creates rights; and second, how the recognition of equality functions to secure rights. What is this *isoi kai omoioi* whose recognition is supposed to constitute rights?

Green's remarks on claims and claiming scarcely provide an analysis of this important aspect of any theory of rights. In fact, he says very little, and what he does say is more puzzling than it is clear. We should, however, examine what he says on this score for whatever light it casts on his view of what rights are. The important allusions to claims occur in sections 121 and 143 of the *Lectures*. The ordinary citizen, he writes, regards the claim he makes for himself "as conditional upon his recognising a *like* claim in others, and thus as in the proper sense a right—a claim of which the essence lies in its being common to himself and others." (121LP, italics added) Not every claim is the object of recognition. The claims which can be recognized are, apparently, "like claims." Moreover, just as not every claim is one of right, i.e., can become a right, so too it is not the exercise of every power that can be *claimed* as a right: "It is not every power . . . that is properly claimable as right. The condition of its being so claimable is that its exercise should be contributory to some social good. . . ." (143LP) Green emphasizes this point by saying that "no exercise of a power . . . can be claimed as a right unless there is some common consciousness of utility shared by the person making the claim and those on whom it is made. It is not a question whether or not it ought to be claimed as a right; *it simply cannot be claimed except on this condition.*" (143LP, italics added)

There are two points to note here. First, a right is a "common" or "like" claim. We have yet to determine what Green means by "like claim." Second, Green seems to be setting down a condition for claimability, though this is not clear. Does he mean that one cannot *claim* in the sense of *assert,* unless one is conscious of something which is relevant in some way to the claim? If he does, the point is debatable at least. But he may mean that one cannot *have* a claim unless one is so aware. He writes, "It is the consciousness of such an end to which his powers may be directed that constitutes the individual's claim to exercise them as rights." (41LP) Now I do not see why one has to be intellectually aware of anything in order to have a claim, though one may have to be so aware in order to claim (a verb). Green may be recommending a definition for "a claim." In this definition a claim is a conscious awareness of an end. But this will not do, for awareness by itself does not imply the existence of a claim.

It is obvious that Green considers claims and claiming important aspects of rights. But what it is to have a claim and to claim is never clearly analyzed. His theory is most frustrating on this score.

What is more important, however, for our purpose here is Green's contention that the claims relevant to rights are "like claims." We should consider this in the light of Green's further contention that the existence of rights in a particular society presupposes that the members of that society regard themselves as equals in some sense. Rights, we are told, are constituted by the mutual recognition by men of each other as *isoi kai omoioi*" (139LP) Here we come upon the third sense of "recognition" in Green's theory, the sense of acknowledgment and respect. It is the sense Green intends when he talks about the "practical recognition" of an I by a Thou in the *Prolegomena.* (190PE) When men recognize each other as *"isoi kai omoioi,* they respect each other, are interested in each other, and treat each other as persons.

It is unfortunate that Green never bothered to translate the Greek terms he employs. He may have intended a sense other than that offered by Plato and Aristotle or, for that matter, Liddell and Scott. We will have to assume for the moment that by *"isoi kai omoioi"* Green intends "equal and alike." The idea is that recognition of equality in some sense is a condition for the existence of rights. Now, does Green mean that rights can exist only among persons whose claims are alike or who claim the same things? He says that rights "depend for their existence, indeed, on a society of men who recognise each other as *isoi kai omoioi*, as capable of a common well-being. . . ." (148LP) Here, to recognize persons as "equal and alike" is to regard each of them as capable of achieving a well-being which can be shared or communally enjoyed. In this sense of "equal," i.e., that each man has an ideal or goal of well-being which is "common" in some sense, does it follow that persons have equal needs, capacities, desires, etcetera? Does the existence of rights presuppose or require some fundamental equality and sameness of persons and claims such as in fact does not exist? Is it not possible that different and conflicting claims and powers can be equally contributory to or constitutive of a common good?

Green's contention that rights depend on the recognition of some sort of equality is vague enough to raise more questions than it answers. It has also compelled some critics to argue that his theory reflects a homogeneous society where individual and social needs and claims coincide inevitably. Green, it has been said, does not appear to allow for diversity and conflict of the sort that exists in fact in the world of real men and real relations.[13]

It is not clear, however, that we need to conclude from Green's commitment to some sort of equality that he was unaware of differences and conflicts and that he does not think they enter into the domain of rights. Actually, the import of Green's thesis that claims of right are like claims and that the recognition of equality is presupposed whenever a claim is recognized as a right is that rights—specifically human rights, for it is these rights he is talking about in the *Lectures*—are *equal rights*. For Green, moral and human rights either are equal rights or they are not rights at all. Moreover, and this is crucial, rights are reciprocal: "All rights are reciprocal as between the person exercising them and the person against whom they are exercised. My claim to the right of free life implies a like claim upon me on the part of those from whom I claim acts and forbearances necessary to my free life." (233LP) One cannot claim a moral or human right for oneself which he is not willing to claim for others or recognize others as having. In a situation where some have rights and others have duties only, there are, properly speaking, no rights at all.

To recognize another as an equal is to respect his ability to secure a well-being for himself. It is not necessarily to view him as being equal and like one in respect of anything else. Green seems to argue that such recognition predisposes one to act appropriately in the face of another's claim. In this sense rights are constituted by the mutual recognition of equality. Rights, for Green, reflect not a homogeneous society but one where there is mutual respect among persons.

Several problems, however, arise in connection with the principle of equal rights and like claims. Green's failure to state this principle clearly and the fact that he does not indicate what he means by "equal" and "like" invite conflicting interpretations of his views and suggest, to some critics at least, that he was unaware of certain important issues and facts which any theory of rights must consider. My own feeling is not that he was unaware but that his treatment of certain topics is incomplete.

Before turning to these problems one point ought to be made clear. Green nowhere says that the "content" of equal rights is the same. The equal right to property, for instance, is not a right to equal property. Property, as a matter of fact, must be unequal: "Considered as representing the conquest of nature by the effort of free and variously gifted individuals, property must be unequal; and no less must it be so conceived as a means by which individuals fulfill social functions. . . . These functions are various and the means required for their fulfillment must be various." (233LP) Green's analysis of the right to property is not more sophisticated than Locke's. It is significant only in that it suggests that the society in which equal rights are admitted is not one in which all goods and services are distributed equally among the various members. Even on his inadequate formulation of the principle of equal rights Green is not compelled to ignore the differentia in individual needs, capacities, merits, etcetera.

To return. The problems which arise are of two kinds: terminological and "pragmatic." The terminological confusion is due to Green's failure to define certain terms. Consider "like claims." Does the phrase refer to claims that are the same? But like claims are not always the same. Claims that are the

same are said to be alike, though claims that are alike are not
usually said to be the same. Individuals may be alike without
being the same. We normally do not say of two people that
they are the same; we do say, however, that they are alike,
and mean by this that they are similar in certain respects.
What about the term "equal"? Green uses the terms "equal,"
"same" and "like" interchangeably with respect to persons,
claims, and rights. This makes it difficult to determine his
meaning.

This terminological confusion compels the following question: Is Green saying that rights presuppose nonconflicting
claims, that they depend on the total compatibility of various
liberties and privileges? The problem is whether Green's talk
of equal rights and like claims allows for genuine diversity and
conflict.

H. D. Lewis has urged that Green is not aware of the fact
that claims and demands often clash. He does not seem to
realize that there is a need for constant adjustment. It is for
this reason that he is able to assume that rights are the same
for all.[14] This view is not wholly correct, for Green does indicate that adjustment may be required: "The admission of a
right . . . [is] very different from agreement as to what the
right consists in"; rights, he goes on, "need definition and re-
conciliation in a general law." (134LP) But, and this perhaps is
Lewis's main quarrel with Green, he does not go on to consider what sort of law or rule can be appealed to, to settle dis-
putes and to determine the content of concrete rights. This is
in fact the "pragmatic" problem which Green does not face or
deal with adequately enough.

It will be argued in a later chapter that Green tried to determine what rights an individual has and how conflicting
claims might be adjusted and reconciled by appealing to the
principle of a common good. He tried, but it is also true that
his attempt was not wholly successful.

Now let us consider the question of who, according to
Green, must recognize a claim. Many philosophers reject the
idea Green seems to have that a simple majority could secure
or deny any individual's human rights in that society. Ross has
argued that if moral rights depended on recognition, slaves
would acquire the moral right to be free "only at the moment

when a majority of mankind or of some community formed the opinion that they ought to be free, i.e., when the particular person whose conversion to this view changed a minority into a majority, changed his mind."[15]

Since this sort of argument is common in the criticism of Green, we should inquire how he acquits himself on this issue. The following questions appear to be relevant: Who must recognize a claim? Is there some critical point at which recognition can be said to be evident? Does "social recognition" mean majority recognition? I am not asking whether this recognition is public *opinion.* I have argued that more than mere opinion is involved in Green's notion. I am inquiring now into the nature and extent of the *public* which recognizes, that is, acts and responds appropriately to the assertion of a claim or power to act.

Critics have assumed that "social recognition" means recognition by the majority. I think this is a mistaken assumption. Green does not imply anywhere that social recognition is solely a function of the majority in a society. As a matter of fact, he sometimes talks as if the relevant recognition can be between "two parties," whether these are "individuals, families or tribes." (134LP) No man has to conduct polls in his community to determine whether he has a particular right or not. Green is not saying anything so absurd. He does not specify any number when he refers to social recognition. Moreover, he writes, "it may be truly urged" that "there is no ground . . . for considering a man's fellow-citizens to be the sole organs of the recognition which is needed to render his power of action a right." (146-47LP) The "needful" recognition is forthcoming from the man who claims and from those acquainted with the action to which he claims a right. The theory that rights are made by recognition does not commit Green to the view that the majority of members in society are the final judges of what powers should be exercised.

But Green does argue as if social recognition is observable in some sense. If it cannot be measured numerically, if it is not a matter of conducting polls, what sort of evidence would count toward establishing that there is social recognition of claims in a society and therefore that there are rights in that society? Who, in other words, must recognize claims? I think

Green would say: "No one in particular but everyone in general." This is perhaps as unsatisfactory as Ross's account, but it comes closer to what Green intends. Social recognition is a matter of "consensus of action," and not a record of individual decisions and opinions. A consensus, even of opinion, is not necessarily the product of a vote. We can determine the consensus in any number of ways, and one of these is to observe whether in a given society there is the sort of activity which is normally taken as evidence of claims exercised and rights enjoyed. We would not have to count any heads or record opinions. I think Green would agree that opinions are not always a mirror of recognition. People in a community may be of the opinion that certain individuals in that community have rights and yet they may fail to respond properly to these claims, i.e., fail to act in such a way as would enable these individuals to put their claims in force.

It may be helpful to quote M. Macdonald, who asks who makes the ethical judgments which concern the fundamental structure of a society. She says that we cannot determine this simply by examining the record of explicit decisions:

For, indeed, the fundamental values of a society are not always recorded in explicit decisions by its members, even its rulers, but are expressed in the life of the society and constitute its quality. They are conveyed by its "tone" and atmosphere as well as by its laws and Statutory Rules and Orders. The members of a society whose values are freedom and equality behave differently, walk, speak, fight differently from the members of a slave society.[16]

If we were to look for social recognition in a society, we would observe it in the way the "fundamental values" are observed, that is, not in opinion polls but in the whole life of the community, its activity, and the general "tone" that pervades it. Is this an acceptable account of what Green intends? Something he says in connection with the right to resistance indicates that we are on the right path: "That general recognition of its exercise as being for the common good, through which the power of resistance becomes a right, must be something more habitual and sustained and penetrating than any vote of the majority can convey." (108LP)

Thus far, we have examined what for Green are conditions

for rights, that is, what must obtain in order for rights to exist. We have seen that rights presuppose a number of factors, among which are persons who are capable of engaging in purposive activity, and communities or societies where individuals relate to each other in certain ways. In this chapter I have tried to elucidate what for Green is one of the most crucial conditions, namely, recognition. But Green never clearly states what recognition is a condition for. It is not enough to say, as he does, that it is a condition for the existence of rights, for rights "exist" in a number of different ways. That is, we speak of *having* rights, *exercising* rights, *enjoying* rights, *asserting, claiming, denying* rights, and so on. In the previous discussion we have not considered whether recognition in the sense of response and appropriate action in the face of a claim is a condition for having or for exercising and enjoying rights. Let us to turn to this issue now.

It is perhaps unfair to raise this issue; Green does not examine it himself in just these terms. It is, however, important to try to decide what his stated view commits him to on this score. We can do this only in an "impressionistic" way in this section, for what Green is finally committed to can be determined only after we have examined his theory of the common good. This is because the recognition which renders powers into rights is itself founded on or justified by a reference to or acknowledgment of a common good.

We may very well agree with Green that rights have a social character or a social basis, where this means simply that rights depend on social relations and can exist only among persons who are capable to some extent of observing certain moral rules. But we may not agree that rights depend on the social situation where this means that they are "real" only when claims are recognized and acted upon. We think, ordinarily, that a right is "real" when it can be "justly claimed." Many philosophers, even those who do not subscribe to the classical natural rights doctrine, deny that recognition in any sense is a condition for rights. This is especially true of recognition in the sense of response and action. Surely, it will be said, slaves and women had rights before societies recognized them, i.e., did anything about their claims. They had rights because their claims were just in the light of certain fundamental principles

of justice and equality to which all rational persons can
adhere.

It seems difficult to maintain that in order for an individual
to *have* a right others must recognize his claim. What if they
do not? Green, as Lewis writes, appears to have been confused
"about the distinction between the condition under which a
right is real and the conditions under which it may be effec-
tively claimed."[17] John Plamenatz also has argued against
Green's view:

There should not arise any question of *recognition* so long as we are
considering merely what powers men or lower animals should have.
Such a question arises only when we come to discuss what powers
they can, in effect, exercise. . . . The theoretical case, none the less,
cannot be upset by this consideration, for the necessary conditions of
a man's exercising his rights are not the same as the conditions of his
possessing them.[18]

The assumption made by both critics is that where Green
argues that recognition enters into the constitution of rights
he means that it is a condition for the having of rights. But, in
fact, Green's position on this matter is not straightforward.
Sometimes Green writes as if recognition is a condition for the
exercising of rights. Thus, he frequently says that it is the exercise of a power that is recognized. (103,31LP) But even
where he maintains this, he goes on to say that unless the exercise of a power is allowed, there is no right. (31LP) And this
is to recommend the somewhat peculiar thesis that one cannot
be said to have a right unless one is allowed to exercise it in
fact. Does Green actually hold such a view? It is hard to determine whether or not he does. If he does, he cannot easily
explain how it is that rights may be denied.

I think Green does blur the distinction between "having"
and "exercising" rights. But while this is problematical in his
theory, it is also the source of an interesting contention. I am
not saying that one can make interesting proposals while ignoring certain canons of clear and logical thinking. I am sug-
gesting that Green does not consider this distinction very important because he contends, apparently, that certain conditions relevant to the exercising of rights determine whether or
not one *has* a right. Green is saying in effect that, if my claim

is conceded and I can act either with my own resources or with the aid of others or both to put that claim into effect, I have a right. If, on the other hand, my claim is not conceded on demand, if there is no appropriate action or response to my claim, if I have to beg or plead for beneficent treatment, then the ..... a real question as to whether or not I have a right in fact

According to Plamenatz, the theoretical case for rights is concer...d only with the conditions of a creature's possession of rights. As opposed to this, the import of Green's thesis on recogn..... is that one cannot ignore or discount the conditions of .. ....'s exercising his rights even when one is trying to deter.....ne what rights he ought to possess.

It is not that such conditions are the only relevant considerations in deciding what rights there ought to be. Green is not saying that one ought to possess only those rights that in fact one is recognized as possessing. Recognition in the sense of response and appropriate action is not a ground for the validity of rights. The rights a man ought to possess, i.e., what claims ought to be recognized, are determined by, among other things, reference to considerations of social well-being or what Green calls "a common good." But whatever rights one does have depend on that appropriate action and response which is forthcoming when one claims or demands something as one's right. In the total absence of such response, what is it to have a right, Green would ask, or for a right to exist?

What is problematical in all this is that we tend to think that even in the absence of such response there are times when we do have a *claim*, we are *entitled*, that is, to whatever we claim, and that this counts for something. It is not clear that we require the appropriate action or response of others in order to be entitled. Green does not appear to appreciate enough that having a claim is an important consideration for having a right, or, more precisely, for determining whether anyone has a right. While there are conditions for having a claim, and Green outlines some of these, it is not true that one of these is the appropriate action and response of others.

Whether or not this objection is met by what Green has to say about the relation of a common good to claiming, we can admit that his idea that rights are made by recognition is neither absurd nor irrelevant to our attempts to determine what it is to have a right. Whether or not it can do the whole job of explicating the concept of a right is another story. It is useful to the extent that it focuses attention on the fact that rights exist where individuals not only demand and claim certain things but also act or respond in certain ways and entertain certain ideals. We are not always aware of this; we seem to think that simply claiming or "claiming justly" is sufficient to establish the existence of a right. But rights—and I would add, moral and human rights especially—are extremely fragile.[19] What it is to have a right or even a claim is not an easy question to answer. The "making" of a right is an extremely complicated affair, and Green's notion of recognition suggests some ways in which rights come to be.

One critic has written that people are "attracted to the theory that rights are made by *recognition* chiefly because they suppose that the general acceptance of it tends to promote law and order."[20] Green is eloquent on the need for law and order; but he also maintains, and as strongly, that the state is justified by the extent to which it promotes and protects individual rights: "The essential thing in political society is a power which guarantees men's rights." (102LP) Rights, for Green, are very important "commodities." They provide a "certain freedom of action and acquisition," and it is this freedom which is a condition of human dignity and awareness of the values and ends which make life worthwhile. (114LP) Green attaches importance to recognition in the sense of appropriate action and response, not because it promotes law and order, but because it secures rights.

CHAPTER 6

The Common Good and Individual Interests

The theory that moral and political obligation is founded on the common good is supposed to be Green's very own. He was not the first philosopher to employ such a conception; but it is true, perhaps, that he more than any of his predecessors argued that the moral and social life of man is regulated by the individual's recognition of a common good. He writes: "There is an idea which equally underlies the conception both of moral duty and legal right . . . which must have been at work in the minds of men before they could be capable of recognizing any action as one that *ought* to be done. . . . This is the idea of an absolute and common good." (202PE)

A great part of the *Prolegomena to Ethics* is given to a discussion of the "source" of man's morality, his readiness, that is, to perform his duties and to acknowledge the claims of others. Green takes great pains to refute the theory of psychological hedonism as an account of the moral life. He offers his own theory of self-realization and the common good as an explanation of why persons readily submit to the demands of morality. In support of his theory Green appeals to a number of metaphysical and psychological considerations which seem to us today neither acceptable nor particularly interesting. Such ideas as the "spiritual principle in man" or the "self-objectifying personality" neither clarify nor advance our understanding of why most people have more than a merely prudential interest in being moral or in pursuing certain ends.

We need not be detained here either by Green's metaphysics or the particulars of his moral doctrine, for his theory of the common good as a psychological account or explanation of the moral life is not essential to his thesis that the common good as an *ideal* determines and justifies rights. It is true that he employed the former account to buttress the latter contention, though we will not examine here whether his attempt was successful or not. We should extract from the moral doctrine whatever is relevant to the matter at hand. This is, to consider how the principle of the common good determines and justifies rights.

Two issues can be distinguished in the moral doctrine, both of which are relevant to our topic. The first is the account of moral obligation; the second is the conception of the *summum bonum*. Various interpretations have been offered of both Green's analysis of moral obligation and his idea of the ultimate good. Since a certain idea of the right and the good underlies the theory of rights, it should be indicated here what Green maintains on these issues. In chapter three a certain interpretation of the *summum bonum* was offered; these remarks will be amplified below. For the moment let us consider Green's account of moral duty and interest.

According to some writers, Green is saying that it is the duty of all individuals to promote a common good because it is a good common to them. His theory of the common good is thus an attempt to reconcile duty and interest. One critic has written: "T. H. Green appears to have laboured under the belief that before anyone could be expected to pursue the common good he must somehow be convinced that he was thereby pursuing his own greatest (net) good."[1] The prevailing idea seems to be that Green does not allow for disinterested duty or disinterested concern about the welfare of others. He appears to think that no one can be interested in another man's good unless he thinks of the other as identical with himself. Further, he finds it difficult to accept the view that it can be a man's duty to promote what is not beneficial to himself. It turns out that Green's theory is as egoistical as that of the cruder hedonists against whom he argued. Since he found it hard to believe that a man can be interested in the good of others, he evolved his theory of the common good to show that men will cooperate to promote a good only when it is common to everyone. A man's duty is defined by his interests, and where his interests are common with others he has a duty to promote a common good.

Now it is true that many of Green's expressions inspire such

an interpretation, but it is also true that this reading is based
on a literal interpretation of a few sentences in Green's work
and an almost total disregard of the major contentions of the
Prolegomena. Green was a disciple of Kant; this should be obvious to anyone who reads the former. It seems unfair and
scarcely sensible to attribute to Green a view of moral obligation which is so incompatible with the main lines of the Kantian doctrine. Even Green's adherence to an Aristotelian conception of the end of man does not attentuate his commitment to the idea that true moral goodness lies in the performance of one's duties whether these are in one's interest or
not.

I am inclined to agree with H. D. Lewis, who argues that
Green neither sought to reconcile duty and interest nor sur-
rendered his belief in the distinctness of persons.[2] Every individual, according to Green, has an ultimate worth. The claims
and interests of every individual are to be counted not insofar
as they are common but insofar as they are compatible. We
will have to return to this matter. For the moment it is important to realize that "common good" refers to a universal end.
"The 'True Good' comes to be represented by Green as a
'Common Good' mainly because it is the pursuit of an end
which is 'universal' and 'necessary' in the way we usually employ these terms in ethics."[3]

Green writes that the common good is an ideal, a *demand*
derived not from observation of what exists "but from an in-
ward requirement that something should be." (230PE) Pursuit
of a common good does not presuppose either the identity of
individual interests or the "oneness" of man, nor does it require that acts of duty or benevolence be coordinate with acts
of self-love. When Green writes that the "distinction of good
for self and good for others has never entered into that idea
of a true good on which moral judgments are founded"
(232PE), he does not mean that we are moved to act benevo-
lently or perform a duty because we desire to please or benefit
ourselves. It is this sentence which has inspired the prevailing
view. Once we have understood what Green means, we shall
see that the usual interpretation of Green's position is un-
founded.

According to Green, the quest for self-realization is characteristic of all moral activity. This is man's "proper" end. This is not to say, however, that self-realization is the "object" of our various desires. We desire various things. Just as we desire or have an appetite for food, so too we desire to be kind to others. Our benevolent desires, like our appetites, terminate upon their objects. When we have achieved what we desire, there is self-realization or satisfaction or pleasure. But, as Green writes, "it is a confusion to represent this as an object beyond the obtaining of food or the doing a kindness, to which the appetite or benevolent desire is really directed." (161PE) Neither benevolence nor any other desire is necessarily a desire for personal advantage or gain. Each desire has its object, and the achievement of this object results in self-realization or self-satisfaction, but the latter is not to be confused with the immediate object of desire.

We have self-regarding wants and desires and other-regarding wants and desires. When we try to determine, however, what we ought to do in any particular situation, we must, according to Green, consider not merely what we desire to do but what is desirable on the whole. In formulating a judgment about a duty one cannot or should not distinguish between what is good for self and what is good for others, because what is really good, and therefore one's duty to promote, is equally good for all. Green writes in the *Lectures* that a man does not always grasp the idea of the good "in all its fulness": "He apprehends it only in some of its bearings: but it is as a *common* good that he apprehends it, i.e., not as a good for himself or for this man or that *more* than another, but for all members equally in virtue of their relation to each other and their common nature." (121LP, italics added)

In calling the true good "common" Green means, in part, that judgments about the good are universalizable and apply equally to all. A man cannot advocate a course of action as good or right which he is not willing for others to pursue. Here, Green is well within the Kantian tradition; he is scarcely advocating an egoistic view. He adheres to the Kantian doctrine insofar as he conceives of the ideal as universal and as having the force of a categorical imperative. But he diverges from this doctrine in that he introduces an Aristotelian element in his theory of the good. He tries to show that the categorical imperative derives from the nature of man and is an end which each individual really desires. I would suggest further that Green ultimately gives a teleological account of moral obligation.

Green does not argue that one has to be convinced that he is promoting his own interests and good in order to pursue a common good. One has primarily to be convinced that this is the right thing to do. What is right may or may not serve the self, that is, coincide with personal wants and desires. But, with Plato and Aristotle, Green does maintain that it is ultimately "in one's interests" to do the right thing, even though there may be times when one is not "interested in" doing the right thing and when acting rightly is not in one's immediate interests. This view, however, should not be confused with the view that a man's duty is only to promote his own interests.

In the foregoing I have been concerned to deny the view commonly attributed to Green that a man has a duty to promote his own interests and that a common good is pursued only to the extent that one is convinced of the identity between his own good and that of everybody else. A common good is pursued because it is a universal good. To recognize such a good is not to opt for strictly personal wants and desires whose satisfaction benefits the self alone. Green's theory of the common good is perhaps an unrealistically altruistic doctrine. This becomes apparent when one examines it from the point of view of the theory of rights.

Without attempting to explain how Green arrives at the idea that recognition of a common good is the source of the moral and social life of man, we shall try to discover how he relates the conception of the common good to rights. By way of summarizing what has been said in previous chapters, it might be well to quote Green:

The idea, then, of a possible well-being of himself . . . and relation to some group of persons whose well-being he takes to be as his own, and in whom he is interested in being interested in himself . . . these two things must condition the life of anyone who is to be a creator or sustainer of law or . . . custom. . . . They are conditions at once of might being so exercised that it can be recognized as having right, and of that recognition itself. [203PE]

Rights require a conception of well-being which is at once a personal and social ideal. If we examine the various rights which Green regards as "fundamental" or "natural," we will note that the *foundation* of each of these rights, though variously expressed in the *Lectures,* is the same in each case, namely, the "capacity on the part of the subject for membership of a society, for determination of the will, and through it of the bodily organization, by the conception of a well-being as common to self and others." (151LP) This is the foundation of a man's right to life and liberty, to family rights, and to various property rights.[4]

Green employs a number of terms and phrases interchangeably when he refers to the "ground," or foundation, of rights. Thus, he talks about "common interest," "social good," "public interest," and "common well-being." He appears to equate the common good with all of these. To recognize a common good is to recognize common interests or ends; to act in the name of the common good is to promote the public interest; to seek the common good is to seek the well-being of all, etcetera. The careful distinctions which have been drawn in some contemporary essays between "public interest" and "common good" as distinct concepts and between "interest," "end," and "good" as terms referring to different things do not occur in Green's work.[5] This lack makes it very difficult to determine what he means by "a common good." The use of various terms to refer to the same thing may imply some confusion in Green's thinking, but it also indicates a desire to locate a meaningful reference for the term "common good." Whatever he does mean by the terms, it is clear that he takes the common good to be the ground of rights of all sorts and the principle according to which various rights are determined and defined. "An individual right," in the words of Hobhouse, who bases his own theory on Green's, "cannot conflict with the common good, nor could any right exist apart from the common good."[6]

There are two powerful strains in Green's theory of rights: first, his insistence on the ultimate worth of the individual, and second, his idea that the individual has no right to anything that is not for the common good. It has been remarked that regard for the common good is, most of the time, a regard for the requirements of social order rather than for the requirements of individual justice. When Green, therefore, argues that rights are determined by a common good, he inevitably sacrifices individual rights to the welfare of the community. The needs of the individual become subservient to those of society, and since the latter is the source of rights, it would appear, according to Green, that society can do no wrong.

These are among the stock objections brought against Idealist and Utilitarian theories of rights in general. Philosophers of these persuasions, writes Macdonald, "though differing in other respects, agree in holding that the rights of an individual must be determined by the needs and conveniences of society as a whole."[7] Now, whatever the problems involved in Green's conception of the common good, he cannot be accused of sacrificing individual rights. To say, as Green does, that rights are determined and justified by a common good is not to imply that these rights are determined by the needs and interests of society. It is easy to draw this inference, but it is unjustified. The common good, as I shall try to show, is an *ideal,* and it is possible that the needs or judgments of *society* are sometimes incompatible with this ideal. Green puts a premium on an ideal, not on society per se. Thus, the human rights of the slave in a society where slavery is condoned remain because the slave, like other men, is capable of communal living. He exhibits this capacity in his relations with a limited number of persons, but this capacity is in principle "a capability of living in community with any other human beings . . . and . . . every such capability constitutes a right." (140LP) In other words, the slave does not have rights because he serves the needs of the society in which he lives, but because his own needs and capacities are elements in the common good, and realization of these capacities contributes to social well-being. (144LP) Society or the majority is not always, says Green, the best judge of social well-being.

On this issue David Ritchie, not T. H. Green, argued that there might have been a time in human history when the existence of slavery was not contrary to what might be considered "natural rights." Slavery may have served a purpose—a need of society—and this being the case, slaves could not be granted the rights of freemen. Ritchie very clearly identifies rights with the needs of society: "The person with rights and duties is the product of society and the rights of the individual must, therefore, be judged from the point of view of society as a whole and not the society from the point of view of the individual."[8] While Green and others would agree that the person with rights and duties is the "product" in some sense of society, it does not follow from this that rights are reducible to the needs and claims of society. Hobhouse and others have commented on the tendency of Ritchie's treatment "to the annihilation of all individual rights even regarded as derivative."[9] But Ritchie's views must not be taken as echoes of Green's. Unfortunately, they have been so taken.

The interesting criticism of Green's theory of rights cannot be developed by concentrating on the stock objections. The main issues are obscured by attending to the question of whether or not Green subordinates individual rights to society. He does not, but he does maintain that rights are "derived" from and "required" by a common good. The elucidation of *this* thesis would seem to be the important matter, and the questions which arise in connection with this are far more complex than the issue of whether or not the individual has rights against society.

It is more fruitful to approach the question of what the common good amounts to as a principle of rights by considering first whether or not it puts a premium on shared wants and enjoyments and withholds value from self-regarding interests and needs or even harmless amusements.[10] This is another form of the question raised in the previous chapter about the nature of "like claims." The issue has to do with the meaning or significance of "common" in the conception of a common good. How important for Green is the *common* factor—whatever this factor is—in determining rights? Cannot people who have no interests or wants in common—or only a few—admit rights among themselves? Is it on the principle of the common good that rights and competition are essentially incompatible? If so, what possible rights does it justify? It would appear that few can be allowed, for most of the welfare rights which Green would consider fundamental are to goods and services for which there is a great deal of competition.

In the sections which follow we will consider the issue of what interests, needs, and functions are relevant to the rights-claims allowed by requirements of the common good. When we have decided what Green's position is on this score, we can inquire how the ideal of the common good can be appealed to, to determine who has rights and what these rights are.

Throughout the *Lectures* we are told, in various ways, that powers and claims are recognized as rights whenever they are viewed as contributory to a common good. A reference to social well-being is involved both in the claiming of a right and in the allowing or granting of a right. The exercise of a right may not be incompatible with social requirements. He who claims a right and those upon whom the claim is made must share "some common consciousness of utility." (143LP) The assertion of any right "must be founded on a reference to an acknowledged social good." (143LP)[11] The requirements of social well-being are paramount. And so it goes.

The question now is: whether and to what extent the reference to social well-being or a common good requires that only shared interests and social wants as opposed to competing interests and antisocial wants be treated as the proper subjects of rights-claims. Is it the point of Green's thesis that on the grounds of a common good, shared or common interests are *preferable* to nonshared interests?

Brian Barry has raised this question in connection with Hobhouse's "principle of Harmony."[12] The argument developed by Barry is applicable to Green's thesis as well; for, as the former maintains, Hobhouse based his own theory on that of Green.[13]

It is argued that the principles of harmony and the common good entail that, one, "harmless amusements which do not contribute to the well-being of others" are without value; two, that a way of living which is not compatible with "social service" should not be permitted; and three, that antisocial wants be ruled out. What seems to be required on this principle is that wants other than those shared not be counted and not be satisfied even though people do actually seek to satisfy them. In Barry's interpretation of the principle of the common good or harmony, those who are pursuing harmless

amusements or those who cannot fulfill a socially useful function are not allowed rights. He takes Green specifically to be
saying that "there is no 'right' to enjoy oneself unless there is
a recognized public interest involved."[14] There is for Barry a
very obvious Puritanical strain in thinkers like Green and
Hobhouse, and where God is not mentioned, "society" has become the guardian of all that is true and good. The principles
of harmony and the common good seem, to Barry, to arise
from an "aesthetic" need:[15]

There may be a certain quasi-aesthetic pleasure to be found in contemplating the idea of a world where nobody sought to satisfy wants
where this was incompatible with others' satisfying their wants: or
even better where all want-satisfying by one person directly helped to
satisfy the wants of others; but this is surely a frivolous reason for
saying that wants other than these should not be counted if people *do*
seek to satisfy them.

It is highly unlikely that writers like Green and Hobhouse
had "frivolous" reasons for advocating their views or for contemplating a world where there was more rather than less
compatibility among individual wants and claims. Moreover, it
seems unfair to treat Green's theory as though it were a plea
for asceticism. But Barry's criticism does raise some important
questions. Three charges must be answered: first, that on the
principle of the common good only shared wants can be the
basis of claims to rights; second, that on this principle only
persons performing socially useful functions can be granted
rights; and third, that on the grounds of a common good, antisocial wants are automatically ruled out, i.e., one cannot
claim a right to satisfy an antisocial want.

Let us consider each of these charges in the ensuing sections.

Does the pursuit of a common good require that persons
seek to satisfy only their shared wants and ignore or suppress
their nonshared wants and desires? It does not seem to me
from what he says that Green must answer this question af-
firmatively. We have noted that the common good, according
to Green, is pursued by means of different objects and in different ways. Many elements compose the common good
—individual interests, enjoyments, and ideals—and not all of

these are shared. Green maintains that both the sanitation worker and the writer of a book on an abstruse subject pursue the common good. But nowhere does he imply that this means that they are satisfying only shared wants. In the very nature of the case the major wants and interests of these individuals are not shared. What is common to the life of scientific and artistic activity on the one hand and that of "practical exertion" on the other is simply that they are both elements in a common good. (288PE) It does not follow from this that these activities or life-styles are characterized by shared wants or enjoyments and that these are what permit us to consider them as elements in a common good.

Green does not eliminate either as valueless or "non-real" the nonshared interests and wants which characterize human endeavor. But it is true that for him not all interests and wants can be the basis of rights-claims. While he does not put a premium on shared wants as somehow superior to other sorts, he does seem to think that, as far as rights are concerned, *compatible* interests and wants are to be given preference. This conclusion apparently follows from the fact that the common good is a good in which each man has a share. The problem then is not whether nonshared wants are allowed but whether incompatible interests, wants, and claims can be recognized as rights.

Just as no intrinsic preference is given to shared wants and interests, so too Green does not explicitly advocate disregard of claims of those who cannot or choose not to perform a socially useful function in the community. Green's view on this point, however, is problematical.

The principle of the common good requires, among other things, that all persons be provided with the means and opportunities to realize their capabilities where the self-realization of one man is not incompatible with that of another. The good is attained in "a social life, in which all men freely and consciously cooperate, since otherwise the possibilities of their nature, as agents who are ends to themselves, could not be realised in it." (288PE) But Green writes also that pursuit of this good is of "general service." (283PE) He implies that the pursuit in various ways of the good serves all. And Green himself wonders whether purely artistic and intellectual activities "serve" in a significant social sense. (289PE) Indeed, it has been urged that Green's view minimizes the importance of artistic and intellectual effort, for he seems to say that there are no purely nonsocial goods.[16]

We cannot achieve any certainty as to what Green believed here because while he raises the question, he does not deal with it directly either in the *Prolegomena* or the *Lectures*.[17] Perhaps his raising of the issue is evidence enough that he regarded only socially useful functions as relevant to rights-claims. I think this conclusion is unwarranted, for what seems to have bothered Green is the matter of "proportion." He does not deny intrinsic value to excellence in the arts, for these too have "a place in the fulfillment of man's vocation." (381PE) But, he writes, "it is a question, so to speak, of spiritual proportion, whether the attainment of such excellence is of importance in any society of men under the given conditions of that society." (381PE) He goes on to explain. In a situation where the fundamental needs and requirements of civil life are not being met, the contributions of the artist would seem to be of little "present" value. They may have potential value, they may survive in history to contribute to the well-being of persons whose fundamental needs *are* being met. But, where people are either starving, or improperly housed, or not receiving the basic services and care which make living possible, the claims of the artist to social support would seem to be misplaced.

We may not like Green's hesitation on this matter. We think that a good song and a good poem are worthwhile even if no one stands to benefit from them. Certainly a man ought to be allowed to indulge his artistic fancy as a matter of right. Green might well concur here. What he seems to be urging is that close attention to the priorities is desirable when an individual is deciding upon a course of action or putting forth a claim. This may or may not be a "frivolous" consideration. It does derive from his belief that all men are entitled to a good life and that everything should be done to secure the good life for all as a matter of right.

If the principle of the common good does not rule out unshared wants and does not, under certain circumstances, disallow functions and activities which are not socially useful, it seems to be true, nevertheless, that it rules out, almost by definition, antisocial wants and merely competing wants.

The question of the place or value of antisocial wants and actions within the framework of a system of rights is large and troublesome. Green's theory provides no final answers. The problem is whether or not he even allows the claim of an antisocial want.

Before we can decide this, we should try to establish some minimal meaning of "antisocial want." This might be done by the use of examples: The desire to park in a place which obstructs traffic because it is the nearest spot is antisocial, as is the desire to play a trumpet at 3:00 A.M. in a suburban home. The desire to strangle one's landlady is antisocial, as is the desire to go to bed very soon after one's guests have arrived for dinner. All of these desires are real and all impart an eagerness to the person who has them. If the reality of these desires and the felt eagerness were sufficient to establish a claim, there would be no problem. We could then say that whenever one really wants or is eager for R, he has a right to R. But we do not usually ascribe rights merely on the basis of wants.

The desires mentioned in the examples above seem to have one characteristic in common: their satisfaction would require the discomfort of others and in some cases would endanger the lives of others. On the principle of the common good in which all may participate there are immediate grounds for arguing against the satisfaction of these desires.

When an antisocial want is such that its satisfaction threatens or curtails the satisfaction by others of their wants, it cannot, according to Green, be allowed as a right. He states: "A right . . . to act unsocially—to act otherwise than as belonging to a society of which each member keeps the exercise of his powers within the limits necessary to the like exercise by all the other members—is a contradiction." (138LP) What Green means is this: If I want to act in ways which are antisocial, i.e., harmful to others, I must be prepared to allow others to act likewise since "a right against any group of associated men depends on some footing of equality with them or with some other men." (143LP) But this is precisely what most people are unwilling to allow. The successful satisfaction of an antisocial want requires that others behave socially and morally. Green's point is, I think, that an antisocial want cannot be the basis of an equal right. A society where there were equal rights to antisocial action would be one in which there were, properly speaking, no *rights* but only powers—in effect, a Hobbesian state of nature. In this sense it is a contradiction, i.e., a misuse of language, to speak about a right to act in a manner which is destructive of the rights of others.

It is true, then, that Green cannot allow the claim of an antisocial want. At this point the following query might be made: If Green does not allow the satisfaction of antisocial desires as a matter of right, has he not missed a fundamental point about the nature and purpose of rights, which is, to secure freedom? There is a feeling that, consequences apart, demands whose satisfaction is not compatible with common or social interests ought to be allowed, for it is individual freedom which is at stake. A theory which cannot accommodate such claims in principle would seem to deny the value of freedom. Green's conception of the ideal which confers claims and rights does not allow for a certain important class of rights, those rights which define the individual's "sphere of autonomy," to borrow from Lamont, whose exercise at the individual's discretion may involve doing what is harmful, antisocial, or even wrong.

The query goes to the heart of the matter of how in the final analysis Green conceived of the common good. Before turning to this it might be well to consider if and how his theory can accommodate merely competing claims. The problems which arise here lead us directly into the issue of the nature of the common good.

Does it follow from Green's assertion that all rights derive from or are justified by a common good and that rights and competition are incompatible? Whether or not it follows necessarily, Green himself seems to have believed that the common good is one "in the pursuit of which there can be no competition of interests." (244PE) While civil society is founded on the idea that there is such a good, most members of any society are prevented from realizing, i.e., enjoying, this good, "because the good is being sought in objects which admit of being competed for. They are of such a kind that they cannot be equally attained by all. The success of some in obtaining them is incompatible with the success of others." (245PE)

What is Green's point in insisting on a good in whose pursuit there is no competition of interests? Indeed, can there be such a good? Finally, what claims or rights can be relative to such a good, given that most claims are competing most of the time? If claims compete for satisfaction, does that mean that they are not elements in, or relative to, a common good?

We have already noted that Green is concerned about certain "personal" or "natural" rights which we today call "human" rights. These rights are distinguished from others in being directly necessary for the achievement of a certain end. They secure "the treatment of man by another as equally free with himself," and they provide for the "free exercise" of the individual's power to make a common good his own. (25LP) What Green means by "making a common good one's own" has still to be determined. But a condition for this is certain rights which are equal rights.

To make a common good one's own, one requires more than mere negative rights, that is, rights to be let alone. Anyone who is a member of a community has such rights, but few men are in fact admitted to the "community of good" in which the goods and services for living the good life are secured to all. The "stream of unrelenting competition" is such that "the good things to which the pursuits of society are in fact directed turn out to be no good things" for many persons in society. (245PE) The rights required by all are "positive" rights or what some writers have called "welfare" rights. And Green seems to have held that the objects to which there are equal welfare rights must be available to all. It appears difficult for him to conceive that there can be competition in an area where there are equal rights. Competition is incompatible with such rights, he believes, and it is these rights which the ideal of the common good confers and which are a condition for its realization.

It has been noted elsewhere that Green does not simply ignore the existence of competing claims. He rather does not allow that such claims can be relative to a common good. He apparently believed that where certain rights are concerned and claims compete for satisfaction, the rights themselves are threatened or violated and the common good is not secured for all.

There is genuine confusion here in Green. He maintains on the one hand that there is a good common to all and that this is noncompetitive, and on the other that the pursuit of such a good varies from individual to individual and is a factor of personal needs and interests. Where interests and needs differ there will be some competition for their satisfaction. Green cannot very well deny this. What, then, is he anxious to deny? It seems that there are certain sorts of competing claims just as there are certain sorts of antisocial wants which cannot be elements in a common good. But in order to discover these we have to examine what the principle of the common good amounts to, what the social ideal is, in the theory of rights.

CHAPTER 7

Rights and the Common Good

I shall attempt in this chapter to arrive at some conclusions about what the principle of the common good amounts to in the theory of rights. Green does not give us very much to go on; he is vague on many issues and the discussion here probably reflects this. Whatever definite statements are made are based on an interpretation which I think conveys Green's meaning. The following questions will be considered in the ensuing sections: First, what, for Green, does it mean to acknowledge or recognize a common good? Second, how does he employ the terms "common" and "good"? Third, is the common good a unitary object or is it the good of all members whatever this happens to be? Fourth, is the principle of the common good an ideal of justice or the good life or both? The final issue is whether or not the principle of the common good is consistent with Green's conception of a "natural" or human right, which he thinks is the fundamental type of right. What sort of common good does one appeal to in the assertion of a *human* right?

It should be noted that in no interpretation of Green's theory would it be true to say that the common good for him is some *metaphysical* entity existing apart from the individual goods and ends of distinct persons.[1] The common good is neither a Hegelian *Geist* informing and shaping the reason and actions of individuals whether they like it or not, nor is it a Rousseauian General Will exactly.[2] It is primarily an ideal, and ideals are entertained by individuals and reflect their needs, interests, and attitudes. Green may have been wrong in thinking that men always attend to the requirements of this ideal when they form societies or other combinations, or that they always refer to this ideal when they acknowledge rights and duties. We may criticize him for this, but it would not be fair to charge him with postulating a metaphysical entity. He is always clear on one point: that the common good is an ideal entertained by individual persons. It is not the good of a corporate being which has a reality apart from its individual members, although "common good" does, for Green, have a corporate meaning. It is not, however, the only meaning it has.

Let us begin this final stage in the reconstruction of Green's theory by examining what he means when he says that a common good is recognized or acknowledged. He insists that rights exist only in a society where there is "a consciousness of common interests" on the part of the members of that society. (31LP) Moreover, as noted earlier, a "common consciousness of utility" is a condition for claimability, according to Green. Recognizing a common good is apparently coordinate with being aware that there are common interests among persons and common benefits. At this point we will not query Green's equation of "good" with "interest" and "utility." For now we should determine whether the recognition of a common good means just awareness of common interests or some more complicated agreement about certain rules and ends.

A. J. M. Milne interprets Green as maintaining that rights can exist only in a society "where there is fundamental agreement." Milne goes on to say that this is an agreement by persons to regulate their conduct according to or in terms of a common good. The common good is a "regulating" principle, and one's recognition of it implies that one will so control and order one's actions as to behave in conformity with it. Recognition of a common good, means, on Milne's interpretation, "an achievement of morality."[3]

Now Green does maintain that the recognition of a common good is the "source" of morality: "Only through a recognition by certain men of a common interest, and through the expression of that recognition in certain regulations of their dealings with each other, could morality originate, or any meaning be gained for such terms as "ought" and "right" and their equivalent." (116LP) But there are two steps in the process of achieving this morality: the first is the recognition of a common well-being and the second is "the embodiment of that recognition in rules by which . . . a corresponding freedom of action for the attainment of well-being on the whole is secured." (117LP) To recognize a common good is not necessarily to frame rules on the one hand or to act as the good man does on the other. One does not become a moral person, according to Green, simply by recognizing a common good. If we take Green to be saying that the mere awareness of common interests or a common well-being renders one a truly moral person as he conceived of this, then it turns out that those who are aware of a common good and who, therefore, can admit rights among themselves, are good people, the kind who do the right thing for the right reasons. But Green denies that moral goodness is a condition for having rights. Moreover, awareness of a common good does not mean a "dominant interest" in such a good. A capacity for rights, he states, is not the same as a capacity for true moral goodness: "It is not indeed necessary to a capacity for rights, as it is to true moral goodness, that interest in a good conceived as common to himself and others should be a man's dominant motive." (208LP) "A *susceptibility* to the claims of human fellowship" (145LP, italics added) is required to qualify a man as a subject of rights:

It is enough if that which he presents to himself from time to time as his good . . . is so far affected by consideration of the position in which he stands to others—of the way in which this or that possible action would affect them, and of what he would have to expect from them in return—as to result habitually, without force or fear of force, in action not incompatible with conditions necessary to the pursuit of a common good on the part of others. [208LP]

The capacity for recognizing a common good which *is* a condition for rights is a capacity for being "considerate" and "mindful" of the claims of others. One does not have to be a moral model of a man in order to be so considerate. The idea is that "a man in his general course of conduct will of his own motion have respect to the common good." (208LP) This respect "entitles him to rights at the hands of the community." (208LP) What motivates this respect does not affect one's claim. One can respect the common good for reasons of self-interest, Green goes on to remark.

When one "recognizes" a common good, therefore, one is

"susceptible" to the other fellow's claims and one has a "respect" for a common well-being. This suceptibility, or respect, is a condition both for claiming and for having or enjoying rights. It is thus a condition also for that recognition, i.e., response or appropriate action, which renders a power of action into a right. In a sense this susceptibility is an achievement in morality, but we must be careful not to take it for more than it is. Nothing, for instance, in Green's analysis prevents us from ascribing rights to a consistent and thoroughgoing egoist. How is this possible? Such a person can *hypocritically* respect or pretend to be mindful of the claims of others. He might in reality be thoroughly amoral; this amorality would not affect his claiming or his asserting of rights so long as he *pretends* to be considerate. Of course, he would have to be a hypocrite at least part of the time, for it is Green's main thesis that rights are possible—that is, claiming and recognizing the claims of others—only where there is general interest in the demands of morality.

To summarize what has been said so far: the person who recognizes a common good, who may therefore claim and enjoy rights, is not necessarily the morally good man in the strict sense of one who acts always with the right motives. To acknowledge a common well-being is not necessarily to commit oneself to the moral point of view. While it is not simply a prudential matter, this awareness of common interests and ends is nothing more than a susceptibility to and mindfulness of the claims of others. This susceptibility is a condition for claiming. The actual enjoyment of rights is secured, however, only when this awareness is "embodied" in rules and there is recognition, i.e., appropriate response, to claims.

Moreover, the person who has rights is not necessarily the fellow who always puts his talents and powers to the best possible social use. This is a point little noted by Green's critics. Green argues in his lecture on the right to property that the power to appropriate certain things should be secured to every individual as a right "irrespectively of the use which he actually makes of it." (221LP) He remarks further, "It is not then a valid objection to the manner in which property is possessed among us, that its holders constantly use it in a way demoralizing to themselves and others, any more than such misuse of any other liberties is an objection to securing men in their possession." (221LP)

Recognition or awareness of a common good does not mean that one will not misuse his privileges and rights. In the passage above Green implies that wherever rights are acknowledged and enjoyed, even on the grounds that a common good is promoted by such acknowledgment, there is no guarantee that persons will not do what is harmful or foolish. Right conduct does not necessarily follow upon either the recognition of a common good or the admission of rights, nor is such conduct for Green a necessary condition for granting rights.

Acknowledging or recognizing a common good, then, amounts to having an abstract sense of justice or being *disposed* to act fairly. On this interpretation of what it means to *recognize* a common good it would seem to follow that seeking or promoting such a good is trying to act justly. It might be objected that Green does not mean just this. The principle of the common good even in the theory of rights is not primarily an ideal of justice. To maintain that it is would be to oversimplify Green's theory.

The objection is apropos. Before we deal with it, however, it might be well to consider briefly how Green employs the terms "common" and "good," for he uses them in such a way as to suggest that the common good has some substantive content which can be specified. If this is the case, then it might be true that the common good for Green does not consist simply in the general disposition to act justly but includes other substantive ends as well. "Seek the common good" then, like "maintain full employment," would describe a determinate goal.[4]

How does Green employ the terms "common" and "good"? A curious appraisal of the phrase "common good" is offered by John Plamenatz.[5] According to the latter the phrase in Green's work is meaningless. His argument goes as follows: We may speak of common *ends* but not of a common *good*. The term "good" refers to a state of mind. Such things as virtue, knowledge, affection, etcetera, which are recognized to be good, are all states of mind and cannot be states of more than one mind. "Indeed," Plamenatz writes, "it is incompatible with the very nature of most of the things which we know are good to be common to two or more persons. For the very reason that they are states of mind, they can be states of one mind only."[6] Green, according to Plamenatz, uses "good" to refer to virtue, and this being the case, the conjunction of "common" and "good" is impossible, i.e., meaningless. Virtue is precisely such that it cannot be common. If it is *my* good, i.e., a state of my mind, it cannot be also *your* good since you cannot have a state of mind which is mine.

I confess to finding Plamenatz's analysis of "good" puzzling. Surely the term is not restricted either by philosophers or by ordinary language to states of mind. When Bentham wrote that pushpin is as good as poetry he did not mean that they were equal states of mind. It will be countered here that what he really meant was that the *enjoyment* felt in playing pushpin is as good as that experienced in writing poetry and that enjoyment is a state of mind. I am not sure that all instances of enjoyment are states of mind (is my cat's enjoyment of the woolly green rug a state of her mind?) Even if this conclusion is granted, there are still contexts in which "good" is not employed to refer to a state of mind. I say to my four-year-old: "Drink your orange juice, it's good for you." Neither the drinking nor the orange juice is a state of mind. I move a piece of furniture and say, "That's a good place for the chair." A place is not a state of mind. We characterize some suggestions as good; I do not know that we would want to say that suggestions are states of mind.

We refer to several kinds of objects as good where "good" has either a subjective meaning or an objective one.[7] An object is good insofar as it is desired or approved by some people; this is the subjective meaning. On the other hand an object may be considered good insofar as it is valuable or desirable; this is the objective meaning. What is good is not always the state of desiring or approving but a specific object which can be anything from a cup of tea to something as vague as freedom.

Plamenatz proposes too narrow an interpretation of "good." Moreover, his view is potentially misleading, for it cannot even be said that knowledge is a state of mind. *Knowing* might be a state of mind, but the term "knowledge" refers to a number of things, including a body of information and skills. Insofar as "knowledge" does refer to the latter, it may indicate something that is shared. The phrase "common knowledge" is surely not without meaning. In Plamenatz's view, however, it cannot be meaningfully employed.

The point to be made here is that there are senses of "good" in which it makes sense to say that the good in question is or can be common or shared. It all depends on the meaning of "common" and "good." It has been remarked that these words have a range of meanings and various possible intermediate senses.[8] As Green employs them, there is no violation of ordinary usage. It is true that he speaks about "common ends," "common interests," and a "common good" as if these were synonymous in meaning; but this indicates only that he failed to distinguish the senses in which an end may be common from the sense in which a good may be common. It does not mean that he did not know what he was talking about, as Plamenatz suggests.

"Good" in Green's work usually refers to ideal objects, i.e., those that are desirable, as well as to objects that are actually desired. Thus, self-satisfaction or self-realization is a subjective good because it is desired and sought by people. On the other hand, social well-being and the objects that secure this are good in the sense that they are desirable or valuable. The good in the case of desired self-realization is a psychological or nonmoral good; the good in the case of desirable self-realization is a moral or intrinsic good. It should be noted that for Green the desiredness of the former is not a ground for the desirability of the latter.

The objects that secure individual and social well-being are various. What a man will consider good, i.e., desirable, will depend on his personal "circumstances and idiosyncrasy." In some cases keeping a family comfortably alive is regarded as good, i.e., is a desirable end; in other cases, "the advancement of some branch of knowledge, or the improvement of public health or . . . 'personal holiness'" may be regarded as good (239PE). Moreover, the *pursuit* of any of these objects viewed as good is also considered good. The meaning of "good" for Green varies depending on the context in which he employs the term. Most of the time, however, it refers to either a desired or a desirable end. This may be a state of character or an external state of affairs, but it is not just a state of mind.

Green's use of "common" in such phrases as "common interests" and "common good" or "common well-being" in the theory of rights has several senses or meanings. Sometimes it has the usual sense of pertaining to the community or of being shared by several persons. Again, a common well-being might be considered a general or prevalent well-being. It also has the sense of "equal," as noted earlier. Finally, "common" sometimes functions as an individualistic word. This is most clearly seen in "common interests" and "common ends." Green talks about interests and ends which are common not in the sense that each individual has the same interests and ends but in the sense that each has and values his own.

In his sophisticated analysis, Alan Gewirth distinguishes between the individualist and corporatist meanings of "common" and the objective and subjective meanings of "good." These are extreme alternatives, and there are various intermediate meanings. Depending on the combinations of various interpretations of "good" and "common," one can arrive at different conceptions of the common good. The point is, as Gewirth writes, that "no one combination of these meanings is uniquely right or wrong; different ones are applicable in different contexts."[9]

The question then might be put: What combination of meanings of "common" and "good" is employed by Green in the theory of rights—what principle, that is, underlies the system of rights in a community? Does "common good" refer to a unitary object, the object or end of a community conceived of as a corporate being? Or does Green give it a more individualist interpretation in which the common good is the sum or aggregate of the goods of individuals? Or is there perhaps a third meaning where the good that is common is neither a corporate good nor an aggregate of individual goods but a subtle fusion of the two kinds?

Let us now consider how Green specifies the content of the common good—if he does. We shall then have a clue as to how the foregoing questions may be answered.

Green's constant reference to *a* common good that is identical for all and his insistence that such a good is noncompeti-

tive have sent most commentators looking for a unitary object
which is *the* common good. Depending upon the interpretation given to Green's idea, the common good emerges either
as a meaningless notion or it is given a sense in virtue of
which it cannot underlie the conception of a system of mutual
rights and duties.

The comments on this matter of W. D. Lamont and Henry
Sidgwick bear close attention, for they represent a serious effort to grapple with the meaning of Green's principle. I shall
first review their remarks and then indicate what I think
Green has in mind. In doing so I shall enlarge upon the discussion begun in chapter three.

Lamont argues that the "common good" may mean either
one of two things: "(a) It may mean some unitary object for
which all the members of a society are cooperating; or (b) it
may mean the good of all members, no matter in what direction the different members conceive their good to lie."[10] Lamont then asks whether rights depend on the pursuit of a unitary object, that is, on interests which are the same in all persons, or on the pursuit of various goods where interests are
diverse but compatible. According to this critic, Green often,
if not always, supposes that the pursuit of a common good is
of a unitary object characteristic of the objects and ends of
voluntary associations where the members have the same interests and the latter are promoted or protected because they
are the same. Human societies, Lamont says, are not voluntary
associations but groups of persons who *find* themselves together and who cherish different interests. The common good
emerges where each individual is secured "as much opportunity as is compatible with like opportunity for others for pursuing those interests which he cherishes, the interests of all not
being necessarily the same."[11]

Now there are in the *Prolegomena* some sentences which
might suggest that the common good for Green is a unitary
object and the common interests which promote social ends
are interests in the *same* objects. It is curious, however, that
the passages Lamont refers to in support of his interpretation
of Green's view, i.e., 233-36PE, contain statements which express a view with which Lamont would concur. Lamont bases
his interpretation in effect on one sentence, where Green

writes that the good "does not admit of the distinction between good for self and good for others." (235PE) I have tried
in a previous chapter to show that this sentence expresses
Green's view that the good is universal. Each man seeks or has
a good. In pursuing whatever is his good each man views it as
good in the same sense of "good" employed by other men.

Throughout this reconstruction we have noted that for
Green the working idea of a common good or well-being varies from individual to individual according to the nature of his
interests. In the passages averted to by Lamont, Green emphasizes this point. But he also wants to establish that the state
of well-being or the good life cannot be constituted by opposition between self and others. Where there is opposition there
is not well-being. This does not mean that the elements of
well-being or the common good are the *same* for all.

In a crucial paragraph which comes at the end of Book III,
where Green summarizes the major points of his thesis regarding the common good, he writes: "Such a good may be
pursued in many different forms by persons quite uncon-
scious of any community in their pursuits." (283PE) Then,
further, "If we would find an expression applicable to it in all
its forms, 'the realisation of the capacities of the human soul'
or 'the perfecting of man,' seems best suited for the purpose."
(283PE) Green insists on this expression not because it indicates a unitary object but because it underscores the point that
the common good is "an object for which there can be no
competition between man and man, and of which the pursuit
is of general service." (283PE)

The common good is equated by Green with self-realization.
In the very nature of the case self-realization is not unitary; it
varies according to individual selves. Green certainly does not
imply that in pursuing the common good everybody is realizing the same self. But he does suppose that realization by diverse individuals of their needs and capacities is, first, a noncompetitive enterprise, and second, a mutually beneficial pursuit. That is, self-realization is a common good in the sense
that it is desired by each individual member of the community
and that the realization by each member of his capacities benefits the community as a whole.

Apart from the fact that "self-realization" is an extremely

vague concept—on Green's own admission as well—can it be maintained that pursuit of such realization is noncompetitive and of general service? It is here that Henry Sidgwick's criticism is relevant.

Sidgwick's penetrating criticism of Green raises a number of problems for the latter's moral doctrine.[12] For our purposes here the comments on the common good as a noncompetitive good are of immediate value. According to Sidgwick, the most attractive feature in Green's conception of the moral end is its noncompetitive character; but, he argues, it is impossible to maintain, as Green does, that the distinction between good for self and good for others has never entered into the idea of true good. Moreover, this view is, Sidgwick maintains, in contradiction to Green's own account of the conscientious man.

If Green means by a common good the realization of human capacities, then the good cannot be noncompetitive, says Sidgwick. He alludes to Green's view that the realization or perfection of human capacities includes efforts in the arts and sciences as well as in moral virtues. Sidgwick's point is that in order to achieve perfection in the arts and sciences one must achieve a certain level of material well-being, and the objects here are competitive.[13] One might be morally virtuous under any external conditions of life, according to Sidgwick (Green would disagree); but intellectual perfection requires special conditions, and the struggle and methods to achieve these are not always compatible with Green's ideal.

Moreover, Green himself does not consistently adhere to the view that the good is in fact noncompetitive. He talks about the conscientious man who is scrupulous not to promote his well-being at the expense of others. This, for Sidgwick, implies that the well-being of one man may consist to some extent in objects that admit of being competed for. Green's own inquiry into the nature of the just man argues against his view that the "true good" is noncompetitive. If it were, a man would not have to take care to act in ways not incompatible or in conflict with the aims and actions of others.[14]

Finally, as self-realization is sought by all men and takes place all the time—for the sinner as well as the saint—it is not clear how pursuit of this can be of general service. In itself it provides no criterion for right and wrong action, especially since it is the sort of thing adverted to by the most vicious natures. One of the deepest and subtlest impulses in certain human beings is the desire for full realization of capabilities and for richness and fullness of life; and this, according to Sidgwick, frequently leads to action which is scarcely of general service. Indeed, some of it is positively evil.[15] Sidgwick's remarks here amount to the assertion that self-realization fails to provide a criterion according to which rights can be determined and distributed.

Let us consider the last point first because Green's theory—on his own admission—seems to fail most conspicuously on this third count. Many have commented on the difficulty if not impossibility of extracting from the conception of self-realization as an ideal *what* rights a man ought to have.

Green argues that the function or purpose of a conception of a moral end is not to yield a code of rights and duties of which men were not aware before they conceived of such an end. (308PE) A philosopher propounding a theory of the good is in no position to dictate actual duties and rights. A definition of virtue, like a proposition of geometry and a rule of law, is a quite different thing when interpreted by living, acting individuals than when entertained merely as an abstract proposition. (308PE) It is the combination of general ethical proposition and interpretation in a particular context which can yield a rule of guidance. The individual is like a judge who interprets a rule of law; after each interpretation new rules emerge which are applicable to new cases.

If Green meets the last criticism at all, it is by denying that moral theory can provide a criterion that determines right and wrong in all cases. Of what practical value is it, then? Green's answer is that a conception of the moral end provides the right questions to ask when one is confronted with alternative actions or rules:

The thought of the intrinsically desirable life . . . of the full realisation of the capacities of the human soul when applied as a criterion for the valuation of the probable effects of action, may be taken to be represented by the question stated in para. 354—Does this or that law or usage, this or that course of action—directly or indirectly, positively or as preventive of the opposite—contribute to the better being of society, as measured by the more general establishment of conditions favourable to the attainment of the recognised virtues and excellences, by the more general attainment of those excellences in some degree, or by their attainment on the part of some persons in higher degree without detraction from the opportunities of others. [371PE]

A theory of rights based on a theory of the moral end would have a similar function, namely, to focus attention on what rights are for and to compel the individual and the community to consider which rights are more fundamental to the better being of society or the good life. Its purpose would not be to provide a ready list of rights.

Green contrasts his view with the Utilitarian conception of the *summum bonum* and finds that the latter is not one whit less abstract than his own. But he acknowledges the "great lesson" of Utilitarianism—that is, "the impartiality of reference to human well-being." (332PE) His own adherence to this precept gives us a clue as to how he conceived of the common good. If Green is attentive to the efforts of the just man, this is not because he thought at bottom that the good cannot be shared or that its pursuit is competitive, as Sidgwick supposed. Green's comments on the ideal of justice are consistent with his view of the common good, as we shall see below.

Finally, to revert to the first of Sidgwick's criticisms (first in *our* order), Green is aware that it may be difficult to conceive of scientific and artistic pursuits as relative to *one* common good which is noncompetitive, but he does not exclude them from the good life. Any goal or activity whose successful pursuit does not require the depression or suppression of other pursuits is an element in the common good.

As I have argued, Green's conception of the good life—a life enjoyed where there is a common good—is, in part, a Greek conception. What characterize this life are *measure* and *proportion*. His notion of self-realization contains an important element of Platonic and Aristotelian psychology. For instance, Green would not allow that the sinner or the voluptuary or the habitual toper is *realizing* himself. He is indulging in excesses which destroy the harmony, or *taxis,* of the soul. We can detect in this view aspects of the Platonic concept of *stasis* which Plato defines in the *Sophist* (227D-228E) as a psychological maladjustment and the cause of intemperance and injustice.

"Self-realization" is employed by Green to imply self-improvement at least, and this would seem to exclude as cases of self-realization the ones to which Sidgwick refers. We may want to argue that Green limits "self-realization" in a manner which is not consistent with ordinary usage. What we cannot say is that his conception is impossible to reconcile with cases of ordinary human endeavor; the self-realization of which Green speaks is a familiar enough human experience. Nor is Green opting for the development of a certain type of personality—an ascetic one, for instance. Neither the saint or anyone else for that matter has priority in his claiming. Anyone whose pursuit of self-realization does not in the very nature of the case exclude the like pursuit of others is a subject of rights.

The main matter is still Green's insistence on a noncompetitive good as an ideal required by rights. Even if everyone is engaged in the "proper" sort of self-realization, there is still competition and competitive claims. Is it Green's contention that where there is competition there cannot be a pursuit of the common good and therefore no rights? If it is, it is surely an unrealistic view and, as Sidgwick argues, eliminates the need for justice. If justice is a set of rules by means of which conflicting claims and needs can be adjusted and served, then in a society where a common good as Green conceives it is pursued, there is no call for justice, for there are no competing claims. Green appears to have a view of the common good which is the good of a society where everyone is a friend to everyone else and, as Aristotle put it, where men are friends they have no need of justice.[16]

I have urged that Green equates the common good with self-realization. The society where social good is promoted is one in which, according to Green, men are "really free—in the sense of being enabled to make the most of their capabilities." (248LP) This being so, Green cannot very well deny the validity of competing claims. He does not, in fact. Green's thesis with respect to the common good as self-realization comes to this: First, insofar as every man is engaged in self-realization, in improving, that is, the conditions of his life and character, he has a good in common with others. Second, insofar as every man is *entitled* to seek his own good in his own way he has a good in common with others. Third, insofar as every individual entertains a conception of the good life he has a good in common with others. In the pursuit of this good there will be competition among particular aims and interests; but such competition, Green is saying, is not destructive of the coexistence of diverse interests and ends. Green is not eliminating competition, though he sounds as if he is. He is saying that the "bestial scramble," to use Broad's phrase, cannot be allowed. Wherever competition becomes a bestial scramble the common good is weakened and rights themselves are threatened if not destroyed; for the bestial scramble, as Hobbes taught, like the society of friends, eliminates the pertinence of justice.

It is not *merely competing* claims that Green does not allow. What *is* incompatible with the common good are *arbitrary* distinctions or claims which violate the principles of justice and equality. When Green writes that the interests or claims relevant to the pursuit of a common good are noncompetitive, he means that they are of the sort whose satisfaction does not require the suppression of other equal claims and interests—i.e., claims and interests which are equally valuable or important to other people. "Noncompetitive" has the force of "nonarbitrary" and "reciprocal" in Green's thinking.

Justice for Green consists in the elimination of arbitrary claims and distinctions. The just man is careful not to try to satisfy a want or a claim which is the sort that cannot by its very nature be pressed by other persons similarly situated, for such a claim is arbitrary. It is its arbitrariness, not its competitiveness, strictly construed, which renders it foreign to a common good.

"Noncompetitive" also implies noncoercing and nonrestraining. The equal right to free life, which for Green is the fundamental right, is consistent with some competition but not with unrestricted or relentless competition of the sort that increases the powers of some and leaves others with nothing.

The key notions, then, in Green's conception of the common good as this is employed in the theory of rights are the notions of reciprocity and the moral community. The notion of reciprocity is at the basis of the ideal of justice; the notion of the moral community is at the basis of the ideal of the good life. If the satisfaction of a claim or want, first, violates the reciprocity of rights, i.e., is a claim which cannot by its very nature be pressed by all members of the community, and there are no just grounds for its satisfaction, and second, undermines the communal sense or respect of an "I" for a "Thou," then that claim for Green cannot be allowed and should not be recognized as a right. Competing claims per se are elements in a common good, but not *unjust* claims, arbitrary or coercive claims, those whose satisfaction threatens the moral community of men—the sort of community in which alone the good life or well-being is possible.

In one sense the good is noncompetitive—the sense in which it can be said that the good life can be made available to all. The good life, according to Green, consists in what one recent writer has called "the maximization of human powers in the ethical sense."[17] The good, then, as *such* maximization, is noncompetitive. But the good construed as "the maximization of utilities or powers in the descriptive sense," to borrow Macpherson's phrase,[18] where unlimited appropriation is seen as desirable and where the infinite desire for utilities is seen as the basis for action, is competitive.

In another sense the good construed as self-realization or the maximization of powers in the ethical sense is competitive insofar as it is true to say that there is competition for the objects which make the good life possible or which enable a man to exert and develop his own powers. So long, however, as this competition does not become a scramble for unlimited appropriation and power *over others* it is compatible with a common good. The common good *is* undermined by the sort of competition which prevails where there is an ideology of scarcity and a concept of man as an infinite desirer of utilities and of power over others. Such competition is coercive and incompatible with the equal freedom of each man to realize his own capabilities.[19]

On the basis of the foregoing interpretation we can say that the common good for Green consists in the realization by individuals of their capabilities in a way which makes possible the moral life or the moral community. The moral community is one in which, as one writer put it, "moral discourse has any use."[20] For Green it is in addition a community of persons with certain value-attributes or attitudes. Achievement of the good life is conditional upon individuals' orienting their individual value-attributes and dispositions within the framework of the community to which they belong. Only then is the *moral* community possible—the one that transcends particular forms and to which all men can belong.

Bearing these rather vague and general statements in mind we can try to summarize Green's thesis on the common good as a principle of rights and specifically of human rights.

The principle of the common good according to which the system of rights in a community is determined and justified is an ideal of justice and the good life. As an ideal of justice it confers rights on the basis of each man's "*suum.*" The common good demands that no "other standard of judging of the well-being of others than in judging" of one's own is applied by every member of the community. (212PE) This is justice conceived of as impartiality with reference to human well-being irrespective of what this well-being is. Green writes that he who is just recognizes others as *isoi kai omoioi* and this recognition is "independent of any theory of well-being on his part." (212PE) Rights, then, are distributed according to each man's "*suum*"; it is crucial that "in the estimate of that well-being which forms the true good each man is to count for one and no one for more than one; that everyone has a 'suum.' " (217PE)

As an ideal of the good life the common good confers rights on the basis of each man's pursuit of self-realization. This pursuit, Green maintains, is of "general service." This too is an important consideration in the conferring of rights. What does Green have in mind here? I suggest that he means something like the following: The person who realizes his capabilities, who develops his powers in the ethical sense, is the sort of person who has certain value-attributes which are characteristically nonegocentric. The "realized" or improved person is, according to Green, the individual who relates his own well-being to that of others almost in a causal fashion. As he writes: "The objects of which a man anticipates the realisation in looking forward to such well-being, are objects, as we have seen, which he necessarily thinks of as realised for a society no less than for himself, for himself only as a member of a society." (235PE) In becoming this type of person a man contributes to social well-being, for his being what he is, is a fundamental condition of the cooperative endeavors and attitudes which make the good life possible for all. In this sense each man's pursuit of his own self-realization contributes to the well-being of all.

How is this characterization of the common good, namely, as a good whose pursuit is of general service, related to rights? For Green, a man's claiming and the rights he is allowed are conditional upon mutual or shared benefits. When he urges that rights "depend" on or "derive" from a common good, he is defending a principle which requires that all the members of a society must stand to benefit by the having and the exercising of the rights in question.

What is the "benefit" that accrues to members of a society by the having and exercising of rights? The answer for Green is: freedom. Rights, he says, secure "the treatment of one man by another as equally free with himself." (25LP) Where there is equal freedom, there is a condition for the realization of what Green calls the "moral capacity," which he identifies as the capacity for making a common good one's own and which I have interpreted as a capacity for membership in a moral community. The mere possession of rights does not guarantee that an individual will make a common good his own, i.e., that such a community among men will be attained. Rights are a necessary but not a sufficient condition for the attainment of this end. The point is, however, that the possession of rights by every member of the community benefits everyone; for rights guarantee an equal distribution of freedom, and this guarantee seems to be one important condition for the achievement of the moral community.

The principle of the common good—an ideal of justice and freedom taken as components of the good life—is thus in Green's theory a distributive and aggregative principle: distributive insofar as it is an ideal of justice or implies the concepts of justice and equal freedom, and aggregative insofar as it is a model of individual and communal good. To seek the common good is in part to act justly or with due attention to the equal claims of others, and in part to promote policies and programs which render more common the goods of society.

"Common good," as Green employs the phrase, seems to have an individualist and corporatist meaning in his theory. It refers at once to individual good and to the good of the community. The good of the individual, i.e., a desired and a desirable end, is the realization of his capabilities; the realization by each man of his capacities is a *common* good, not in the sense that each person realizes the same self but in the sense that each individual has and values his own development and well-being. The good of the community is a common good in the sense that it consists in the sort of value attributes or qualities of individuals which render them members of a moral community—i.e., persons who pursue their own ideals in ways that are conducive to the general pursuit of ideals in society and the achievement of private and common goods. Rights are a condition for the realization or development of these attributes and qualities. When Green says that rights are "for" a common good or "promote" a common good, he means that the possession and exercising of rights benefit both the community as a whole and each member insofar as they provide at least one important element in personal and social well-being, namely, equal freedom.

Freedom is conceived of by Green not merely as a liberty from restraint. In his lecture on "Liberal Legislation" he argues that freedom is a dyadic relation; one is free *from, to do,* or *to become.* He writes: "We do not mean merely freedom to do as we like irrespectively of what it is that we like. We do not mean a freedom that can be enjoyed by one man or one set of men at the cost of a loss of freedom to others. . . . We mean a positive power or capacity of doing or enjoying something worth doing or enjoying." Again, "The ideal of true freedom is the maximum of power for all members of human society alike to make the best of themselves." (W.III.373)

This is Green's celebrated notion of "positive freedom"; his conception of the common good is built upon a principle of freedom. It is obvious that the sort of freedom Green prizes is not the kind consistent with a "laissez-faire morality." The ideal of the common good which confers rights will not allow the sort of claims which violate the principles of justice and equality. Moreover, the type of activity which is allowed as a matter of *right* must be the sort which is "worth doing." What is worth doing must be decided by the individual within the framework of the moral community.

It has been remarked that Green does not have a conception of nonmoral worth.[21] I am not sure about this; but I do believe that as far as rights are concerned, i.e., freedom to do that which is worth doing, the latter for Green is not determined solely by appeal to strict moral considerations. The overriding consideration in deciding the worthwhile X to which one can claim a right is the well-being of all, and this is not merely a state of *virtuous* being. One's rights are not simply to those actions sanctioned by moral rules, for rights are not solely a condition for right conduct.[22] On the other hand, rights as well as the ideals that confer them are a matter of moral significance since they have a basis in moral feeling.

If rights provide freedom, then it follows that rights constitute a common good. Whether or not Green actually says this, it is true, nevertheless, that the whole tenor of his discussion in the *Lectures* points to such a view. Rights constitute a common good insofar as they are a condition for the general well-being (206LP), and a society where a common good is recognized is one where certain rights are acknowledged and respected.

Certain rights are fundamental for Green in the sense that they are prior to and conditions for other sorts of rights. These rights Green calls "natural"; and they include the right to a free life, to property, and various family rights. He argues that these rights belong to every man in virtue simply of his human nature. (155LP) It has been said that this view is contradictory of the main doctrine urged throughout the *Lectures,* namely, that rights inhere in persons only in that they are members of a community.[23] Actually Green does not attenuate his main doctrine, though we may not be satisfied with the manner in which he includes human rights within the framework of his theory. He writes: "The admission of a right to free-life on the part of every man, as man, does in fact logically imply the conception of men as forming one society. . . ." (154LP)

In any community the rights of the members are claims *on* the community for freedom to pursue ends which are elements in a common good. Now, Green writes, "if the claim is made on behalf of any and every human being, it must be a claim on human society as a whole, and there must be a possible common good of human society as a whole, conceivable as independent of the special conditions of particular societies, to render such a claim possible." (154LP)

Human rights, according to Green, require a conception of the good life for mankind. He does not, however, elaborate this conception, nor does he indicate in what sense it can be said that all men form a human society or community. We may conjecture about what he had in mind on the basis of the interpretation we have given his main thesis.

First, the human community is a moral community. It is not the sort whose membership can be determined numerically or geographically. "Moral community" refers to what Green calls "human fellowship." Every man insofar as he is a member of a particular community is a member of this larger, vaguer community in virtue of "the qualities that render him capable of any fellowship with any other men." (151LP) In the sense, then, that all men are capable of human fellowship to some extent, they can be said to "compose" a human or moral community. The moral capacity which for Green is the "foundation" of certain rights is this capacity for human fellowship—for living in some form of community with others. (140LP) Such a capacity does not imply that a person who claims certain rights will behave always in a morally exemplary way. The individual who is capable of human fellowship *knows* the meaning of what it is to behave morally, justly, or in the pursuit of higher ideals. And to be aware of these things is to be a member of the moral community of men.

Second, the common good of human society as a whole is not unlike the good of particular societies. The good which is the object of "a universal society coextensive with mankind" is like the object of particular societies in at least one important negative aspect: it is not "anything which one man or set of men can gain or enjoy to the exclusion of others." (286PE) All men have a share in this more general good.

A human right is a claim to the goods of life which all men

irrespective of their particular communal membership value and can enjoy; it is a "claim of all upon all for freedom and support in the pursuit of a common end." (286PE) Human rights are fundamental to other rights because they enable a man to act as a moral being, to pursue ends or ideals which promote human fellowship or, as Green puts it, "an ever-widening social union in which the claims of all are acknowledged by the loyal citizen as the measure of what he may claim for himself." (283PE) It would seem that this "ever-widening social union," or the moral community, is for Green the common end or good of man. The realization of this end justifies the existence of rights.

CHAPTER 8

Critical Notes on a Theory of Rights

The discussion which follows is an attempt to assess certain aspects of Green's theory of rights. I have been urging all along that the latter is an important contribution to our understanding of the nature of rights. The critical remarks below are not meant to attenuate this view but rather to locate the problematical areas in the theory where further work needs to be done.

It is an incomplete theory in many respects. Green does not deal with some issues which loom large in the contemporary philosophical treatment of rights. He does not, for instance, analyze the intricate relation between rights and claims, nor does he comment on the correlativity between rights and duties. He alludes to this correlativity but does not indicate how it may be employed to elucidate the concept of a right. He is not concerned with the linguistic forms of rights-talk—how, that is, we are to interpret statements in which the expression "a right" occurs. These matters are considered important today.

On the other hand he does raise issues which are little noted today, which are considered "old-fashioned" topics but which, I would urge, require the renewed critical attention of philosophers. My own recommendations derive from a belief that an adequate philosophical exploration of the issue of rights requires the "marriage" of several approaches: Green's ideological approach and the contemporary analytical method, as well as the investigations of jurists and sociologists.

Throughout this review I employ the term "rights" without always indicating the sort of rights to which my remarks are applicable. For the most part and unless otherwise indicated the subject of these notes is the set of human rights which Green and others have called "natural." But I am not concerned here except indirectly with how the adjective "human" functions in the concept of a human right nor do I discuss the various distinctions which have been drawn between human and other sorts of rights. The problems I deal with in a limited way have to do with what the existence of certain rights presupposes (and here I do not always distinguish between legal and moral rights) and how these rights are justified.

In the previous chapters I have tried to bring together in some coherent form the various parts of Green's doctrine. This is the main thrust of what I have called the "reconstruction" of the theory of rights. It may be objected that the latter has been given a coherence which in fact it does not possess. It may be urged further that the theory such as it is leaves too many blank checks for us to be sure of what it amounts to. It appears to be a "program" rather than an "achievement."

There are two possible replies here: In the first place Green's theory is consistent; I have not had to fill any logical gaps. Indeed, the possibility of a reconstruction depends on there being some internal consistency in the theory. But the doctrine on rights is diffuse; it is spread out among Green's theories of political and moral obligation. It needs to be reconstructed so that the various theses on rights may be brought together and their relationships explained and defined. This is what I have tried to do. To the second objection the following considerations may be relevant: whether or not a theory is an achievement is a difficult issue to decide. One wonders about the "objectivity" of judgment here. What renders propositions A, B, C, a "program" and C, D, E, an "achievement" is not easy to decide apart from how we envisage and specify a particular problem or issue to which a theory is directed. It is more fruitful to ask whether Green raises and considers the important issues which a theory of rights must examine. Again, there is no final agreement as to what these issues are.

Most writers would maintain that a normative theory of rights should attempt to answer the following questions at least: What are rights? Who has rights? What sorts of rights are there and how do we distinguish between them? What makes rights possible? How do we justify rights, and do we justify all rights in the same way? The matter is not exhausted by these questions. Concepts of freedom, equality, justice, and law are related to rights and a theory may consider, for instance, how rights achieve or constitute freedom or in what sense rights are equal if they are or what rights can be demanded as requirements of social justice or finally how law is a source of rights. But it is obvious that if a theory does direct itself to these latter issues it is primarily in order to answer the above questions. These are among the fundamental questions, then, and it is fair to say that Green does consider the significant issues as far as rights are concerned. This is an achievement of sorts. On the other hand his treatment is frequently incomplete and in places inadequate. Insofar as this is true his theory is still in the nature of a program.

But this is not to imply that we cannot be certain of what it amounts to. One purpose of the reconstruction was to show that it is possible to achieve some understanding of what Green has in mind without a "radical restatement" of his doctrine. We can also determine what his theory amounts to, where "amounts to" means admitting of explication, interpretation, or evaluation.

The possibility of *this* enterprise—namely, reconstructing, i.e., formulating and explicating Green's theory in his own terms—has been questioned by some writers. An assumption common in the literature, especially in those writers whose reading of Green was influenced by the lectures of Prichard, is that a full understanding of Green's theory of rights and obligation requires a radical restatement of his views. We cannot reconstruct unless we restate, which in effect means rewrite. It was Prichard's idea that we cannot even begin to know what Green is talking about until we restate his doctrine so as to make it available to our ordinary way of thinking. The presupposition here is that the doctrine is not so available, that it is hidden in some mystical linguistic garb, that Green merely *appears* to be analyzing our ordinary convictions about rights but that in fact his language is a disguise for some fairly extraordinary views. When we "translate" his statements, we discover how extraordinary and even queer his actual position is.[1]

My reconstruction is offered as a denial that, one, we have to radically restate Green's doctrine, and two, that his views are in any way strange or strained. I do not deny that it is difficult to fathom his meaning sometimes. We have to interpret this meaning. He is often obscure and so we have to explicate. But the problems that exist in the theory of rights do not derive primarily from Green's failure to employ language in the ordinary way. There is nothing "extraordinary" about Green's use of such terms as "person," "right," "recognition," or "common good." To suppose that there is, is to entertain the illusion that one definite sense can be ascribed to these terms which we are entitled to call their "ordinary" sense. There are many terms in a language which are forensic, whose meaning can be debated. It happens that a theory of rights typically employs such terms. Their meaning is not always to be located by appealing to ordinary language as a criterion. If Green does not choose to attach a certain meaning to a term or concept, it is no argument to say that he ought to on the grounds that this is the meaning ordinarily understood or employed, for this is by no means clearly determined.

Green's views may or may not be correct, significant, etcetera; critical analysis must establish this if it can. It will not do to toss them out as being totally at variance with views ordinarily held by reasonable men. While it has been almost canonical since Moore to reject Idealist theories because of the supposed linguistic fog which surrounds them, I think that *this* form of criticism is often a subtle way of burking rather than resolving an issue. In effect what has happened to the problems Green raised in his social and moral philosophy is that they have been shelved in a case marked: "not-the-ordinary-language-variety." Another purpose, then, of the reconstruction was to salvage Green's thesis both from restatements of various kinds and from the accumulation of dust, for I am not sure that anyone at this point has a privileged access to the final meaning of "claim," "right," and the rest.

We are confronted in the philosophical literature with many kinds of analyses of rights. The emphasis is not always the same. Where one writer will be concerned with the inalienability of certain rights, another will focus on the correlativity between rights and duties. By and large, however, as Melden notes, the concept of a right has been treated as largely derivative. Thus, many important aspects of rights have not been examined.[2] It is precisely for putting rights in a wide context and for bringing to light considerations such as the role of the community and the relevance of operative social and moral ideals in the conferring of rights that Green's theory is interesting and important.

For Green, rights can exist and acquire a significance only within the framework of a community where personal ideals coincide to some extent with the demands of social morality and justice. The problems which arise and require further analysis derive from *these* contentions, not from Green's misuse of language. It is worthwhile to look at some of the troublesome areas in detail.

Before turning to this examination it might be well to summarize the main points in the theory. There are two distinct but related theses: one is an analysis of the conditions required for the existence of rights, and the other presents reasons or grounds why certain rights ought to be secured to all men equally. The two theses may be stated as follows:

Thesis A: Conditions for the existence of rights:

1. The existence of persons who have conscious needs and purposes they wish to fulfill and pursue.

2. The existence of a community whose members acknowledge a set of common interests and purposes which they conceive of as composing a common good. This is, further, the sort of community where there is a susceptibility on the part of persons to each others' claims and a readiness to acknowledge these claims.

3. The occurrence of some appropriate response and action in the face of a demand or claim—what Green calls "recognition."

Thesis B: There ought to be certain equal and reciprocal rights not just among members of a specific community but also among all men irrespective of their particular communal membership because:

1. These rights are a condition for self-realization and the development of a moral community among men of which all men are potentially capable. (To realize the self *is* to participate in the formation of a moral community.)

2. The good life is achieved to the extent that such a moral community is developed and sustained. (The moral community is defined vaguely by Green as an ever-widening union of cooperating and morally accountable human beings.)

The problems which arise in connection with the contentions of Thesis A have to do with Green's view of what it is to be a person and to have an end or goal, as well as with his conception of the sort of society or community where rights are likely to exist, i.e., be acknowledged and respected. Further intricate issues appear with the crucial problem of recognition.

It has been argued in a previous chapter that Green does not limit rights to persons where "person" means a being who possesses a good will.[3] But he does think that a condition for the presence of rights is the existence of human beings who are capable of engaging in purposive activity, who can project ends or goals for themselves. The objects and interests pursued form, so to speak, the content of rights-claims. So far so good. But there is something troublesome about what might be called the "overtones" of the concept of the moral personality and the moral end.

It does sometimes appear as if the moral personality as Green sees it is the *unwavering* personality, the man who has before him a clearly defined end, whose personal ideals are unchanging, and who is steadfast in their pursuit. Green's view of human nature is highly reminiscent of what Macdonald has called "the Aristotelian dream of fixed natures pursuing common ends."[4] This is especially true when Green describes "the end of man" as self-realization. The implications of this for the existence of rights are not altogether clear. Is it a specific, i.e., unambiguous, self each individual tries to realize? There is a suggestion in Green's conception of the moral personality that the self of the citizen, the father, the artist, all of whom claim rights, is determined and fixed in its main traits and all it requires is development and improvement. If Green wants to say that it is this sort of unwavering personality which is a condition for rights, it is not certain that this condition can be satisfied nor that it is a requirement for the existence of rights.

The "self" is constantly being defined and redefined. That is: People project various images of themselves and of ideal forms of life. Within the individual person there is often an array of different and conflicting images of self and outlooks on life.[5] A man's "real" or "true" self is often unknown to him; the seeking which compels rights-claims may be as much for this as it is for ways and means of realizing or developing his capacities.

It is true that a person's interests and needs and ideals figure in the claims he puts forth. Green is right to insist on the intimate connection between purposive activity and the existence of rights. There is also a "common core" in human nature as well as in the individual person. We need not lose sight of the forest for the trees. But Green appears to isolate one dimension of the human personality and to ignore the rest. Perhaps the trouble lies in the use of the term "moral" to describe the personality which is the subject of rights. The meaning of "moral" in this context is not clear. It was suggested in an earlier chapter that the term implies "purposive." Perhaps Green means more. He suggests that the moral personality is the one capable of a certain kind of activity, what I call the unwavering, steadfast kind, with an eye firmly fastened on a common good. This is the personality which belongs to a type of individual whom I will call the "insider," i.e., the goal-oriented fellow, the community-minded man whose life is relatively free from moral perplexity. But there does exist a type of individual whom we can call the "outsider," who is disoriented, who does not always know who he is or what he wants. His life is full of perplexity; his interests and desires clash. Now, and this is the point, no one person is exclusively an insider or an outsider; we are all a little bit of both and it is as such persons that we are conditions for rights. For rights require not only purposive activity but a diversity of goals and a clash between interests and demands.

The facts about persons and the human condition which set the scene, so to speak, for rights-talk are varied and not easy to specify. What it is to be a person—i.e., a claimer of rights and one for whom rights can be claimed—has to be analyzed. The ultimate case for rights, how we justify them and which rights we allow, relies heavily on the correct statement of this condition for rights.

The sort of person and the kind of personal activity Green regards as conditions for rights are too narrowly conceived, and the same criticism can be brought against his view of the society or community in which rights can exist. There is in

Green's discussion the notion that rights require close social ties. His insistence that society itself is a product of the individual's interest in a common good commits him to a view of society whose predominant features are, first, an intense interest in and attachment to a set of common values, and second, a profound social cohesion. The sort of society Green thinks is important for rights seems to be best exemplified not by ordinary civil societies but by special types of social groupings such as tribes, sects, or communities created by blood ties.

The prevalence of common sentiment and agreement in ordinary societies is the exception rather than the rule. If such sentiment exists, it is evinced only in special crises and then one cannot always tell whether there was common agreement all along or whether it was generated, so to speak, to meet the crisis. Yet the fact remains that there are rights—rights are conceived and asserted—in civil societies where, as Edward Shils has pointed out, the attachment to a "common set of values is normally moderate, lukewarm, sporadic and intermittent."[6]

Green again has focused on an important condition for the existence of rights, but his zealous attention to this is somewhat misleading. The important idea in his theory is that rights presuppose some agreement and some fairly sustained interpersonal communication. Unless interests and demands are expressed or communicated there is no occasion for rights-talk.[7] Depending on the nature of the claim, the enjoyment and perhaps even the meaningful assertion of a right require either the positive assistance of another or noninterference, neither of which is forthcoming unless a demand is expressed. The other requirement is also important: unless there is some common ground on which divergent interests and purposes can meet, rights-talk remains pragmatically empty. There has to be some agreement, however sporadic, if rights are to exist, and the community where common ground is located is, in this sense, a condition for rights.

Green's concentration on these factors, however, has obscured for him another element in virtue of which society becomes the "scene" of rights. This is the factor of conflict. Unless demands clash there is no need to talk of rights. Society is typically the arena of conflict between individual demands and is therefore in this further sense a condition for rights.

It is because men are neither angels nor devils—to borrow from Hart—that society with a legal system of mutual forbearances is both necessary and possible.[8] To borrow further from Hart, the fact that men are vulnerable and approximately equal and are possessed, as he writes, of "limited understanding and strength of will,"[9] gives societies their tone and constitutes the psychological basis of most systems of law and morals. I would add that this is a basis also for a system of rights. Men, unlike angels, compete and clash over the satisfaction of their needs and demands; they will call upon their rights where they seek to protect their interests or be free from the interference of others.

Human beings may and often do evince an interest in and desire to cooperate for a common good, but this is by no means the dominant motive behind their various social activities as Green supposed. Nor is this what prompts them ordinarily to seek the protection afforded by rights. It is interesting to note in this connection that some legal systems afford protection first to self-regarding ends and interests and then to mixed or other-regarding ends and interests.[10] This is to say that the claim of the individual to promote his own good whether or not it happens to be anyone else's good is given priority in the matter of legal rights. The law, then, takes cognizance of the selfish motive in human affairs. I do not know whether it would be true to say, as Lamont does, that the law "prefers" this motive, but it *is* alert to the reality of selfish drives.[11]

In a universe where everyone was other-regarding and altruistic there would be no need to ascribe or assert rights. Rights-talk becomes meaningful only where human beings clash and conflict as well as cooperate to some degree.

Sometimes Green says that a susceptibility to the claims of the others is the condition required by rights. Here I think he is on firm ground. But other times he sounds as if the conscious and sustained effort on the part of members of a society to promote common interests and ideals is what is required. This is not true. In general, while I think Green was aware that demands may clash, I am not convinced that he appreciated enough the importance of conflict for a system of rights.

Let us turn now to Green's thesis on recognition as a condition for rights. This raises a number of problems which must be examined even if solutions are not immediately forthcoming. Some preliminary problems revolve around the interpretation of the concept of recognition, i.e., what "recognition" amounts to and whether or not recognizing a claim automatically secures a right where "secures" means that a right is respected, can be exercised and enjoyed. According to Lewis, "it does not follow that in claiming right treatment for ourselves, we recognize the claims of others in the sense of undertaking to respect them."[12] There is often "deliberate wrong-doing," and on Green's account of recognition it is hard to see how this is possible. He seems to be little aware of what one writer has called "incontinence" in respect to rights.[13] There are societies where, even though the rights of certain persons are acknowledged, there is, for some reason or other, no general respect for, or protection of, or noninterference with, the exercise of those rights. It does not seem therefore that recognition always and necessarily secures rights.

As I have interpreted Green, the answer to these charges would be that wherever there is no respect for or protection of the claims of others there is no recognition of these claims. There may be a gesture in the direction of recognition or simply an intellectual acknowledgment but not recognition as Green understands this, for the latter means *appropriate response and action.* Green can also account for deliberate wrongdoing, for he can say that a *claim* ought to be recognized as a right. There is deliberate wrongdoing in the case of the slave whose claims and interests are not recognized by the state and the law. Even private persons may be guilty of wrongdoing, for they may fail to respond appropriately to a demand which is put forth and which ought to be recognized. Green does not say that we always in fact recognize the claims of others whenever we ourselves claim. The extent to which we do, however, determines whether or not ours is a claim which can or should be honored—i.e., whether we do in fact *have* a claim.

But it must be admitted that Green's view is not wholly satisfactory on this score. He does not specify who has to recognize a claim in order to render it a right. One is tempted to ask whether there has to be a "crucial" person or group whose recognition secures rights, very much like the "crucial experiment" which confirms a physical theory.

Consider the case of the slave with which Green himself deals: he tells us that the slave is recognized as free by those with whom he shares a common language and the ordinary experiences of living. These persons act appropriately in the face of his claims. Suppose, however, that the law in a society where there are slaves expressly forbids all forms of communication between the citizens and slaves, and while there is a desire on the part of the former to recognize the claims of the latter, persons are prevented from doing so through fear of legal consequences. What then? Does the slave have a right or doesn't he? Green's answer that the law cannot prevent the slave "from acting and being treated, within certain limits, as a member of society" (140LP) is wishful thinking. There is abundant evidence that the law unhappily can prevent a number of things. Perhaps Green means to say that the recognition by the slave's brother or father is enough to secure his right. If so, we are faced with the question of *who* constitutes the community in which one's rights can be said to exist. The slave's immediate family is in the jargon of psychology an "ingroup." Is it a community?

We must remind ourselves that the subject of Green's theory is natural, or human rights. In the context of such rights does it make sense to appeal to the recognition of an ingroup? One has a human right against the whole world, so to speak, and not merely against one's immediate family. The recognition that is relevant to a claim which forms the content of a human right must be forthcoming from the stranger as well as the brother. It is the human community that counts here, and Green has not specified the range of recognition nor how this can be expressed in the framework of all the factors which constitute the community.

The existence of all sorts of factors conspires both to "make and break" rights. Green has attended to some of these but has failed to consider others. To make his a viable theory a great deal needs to be done, especially with respect to the factor of the community and the notion of recognition. I think Green's theory requires development along the following main lines: First, since the claim is made in a nontrivial sense that the community is the "place," or forum, for rights, we must specify the components of the community in virtue of which it is asserted that rights *require* the community or *derive* from communal and social relations as well as ideals entertained within the community. We need to know how the various constitutent elements of the community, such as rules, institutions, and resources, are related to the existence of rights. The rules men obey or feel obliged to obey and the institutions they foster or wish to create as well as the resources available to them all comprise "the community" and thereby figure in determining whether and what rights will be claimed and admitted.

Who are the members of a community—what determines membership? This is an important question. There are many debates around the issue of what constitutes a community or society, and it does not seem as if the latter can be defined solely in terms of the degree of social cohesiveness or the unity of purpose that exists. If a man is at odds with his fellows, does he thereby cease to be a member of the community? We normally think not.

A theorist who wants to say (and I agree with Green that it is correct to say) that rights cannot exist apart from the community or society must decide what it is about the latter which makes it a *sine qua non* for rights. The matter is further complicated when we want to say that the community in some sense is a condition for human rights. What sense of "community" is intended here, and how do we specify the relation between it and human rights? It may be that we cannot proceed to answer these questions unless we invest the notion of a community with a certain moral import.

The second area which requires development is Green's idea that recognition *makes* rights. Several aspects of this idea need to be analyzed. There is first of all the conception of a right which underlies this thesis. For Green, a right is not simply an entitlement. As a matter of fact, as was noted in an earlier chapter, Green does not attend sufficiently to this side of rights, i.e., as entitlements. The nucleus of a right for him is "power." It is not certain whether he has moral empowering in mind. In any case this view of rights has been criticized. While I do not wish to pursue this matter in any detail I will note the following: On the one hand it is misleading to equate rights with powers if this means that whoever has a right also possesses the power to secure whatever it is he has a right to. It is by no means true that the right itself yields the power to do or prevent. But on the other hand I do not think we can wholly separate the concept of a right from that of a power or capacity, for rights do imply powers in some sense. Jurists are aware of this, more so than philosophers.[14] This may be because the former deal primarily with legal rights and the power of the law may be said to be the core of such rights. But if an individual has a moral or human right, he does not merely have a "sphere of autonomy";[15] in a very important sense he can in virtue of his right exercise some control over the actions of others with respect to this sphere of autonomy, even if this control takes the minimum form of moral censure. The talk of rights as powers is not misleading to the extent that it focuses attention on the intimate connection between individual claims and what can be done to secure them as rights. The fact that this connection may not be immediately evident and may be difficult to analyze should not tempt us into ignoring it away.

Whether or not Green is justified in equating rights with what he calls "recognized powers," this view underlies the most interesting and problematical contention in his theory. There is in effect a weaker and stronger thesis with respect to recognition as a condition for rights. The weaker thesis is not the interesting one, for this amounts to the assertion that recognition is a condition for the exercising of rights and this is not a troublesome view. It is the stronger thesis which is problematical, for here Green seems to be maintaining that recognition in the sense of appropriate response and action is a condition for *having* rights. Green nowhere actually says this, but it is implied when he writes that "without this recognition or claim to recognition there can *be* no right." (31LP, italics added)

Green's strong thesis may be formulated in the following

way: in order for rights to exist, certain conditions must be satisfied which make the meaningful assertion of these rights possible. This seems to me to be the essence of his recognition theory as well as of his idea that rights can exist only within the framework of a community. This thesis requires explication. While it has been alluded to in an earlier chapter, I shall now examine it further because, first, the main lines of Green's theory of rights stand or fall with the plausibility of this supposition, and second, it seems to merit attention independent of Green's theory.

The thesis I am attributing to Green is not to be confused with the view that recognizing, i.e., *knowing*, that one has rights and actually asserting them are necessary conditions for having them. This is an altogether different supposition and a highly debatable one.[16] One can have rights without knowing this and without knowing what they are and what the conditions for having them are. In fact, most persons need to be instructed in these matters. This need does not mean that until such time as they do become aware of what their rights are and actually assert them or insist upon them they do not have them. If it were true that asserting was a necessary condition for having rights, then we would have to say that the world's "silent majority" is without rights. Indeed, only the vocal few would be possessors of rights.[17]

Knowing that one has rights and actually asserting and exercising them are not necessary conditions for having rights. But the truth of this has led many philosophers to suppose further that the conditions for having rights and those for asserting and exercising them are wholly different and distinct. It is in this further supposition that a great deal of trouble lies. It may be that we cannot reduce the one set of conditions to the other, especially where we are dealing with moral and human rights. But maintaining a clear-cut distinction and insisting that one set of conditions has no bearing on the other seems to involve us in paradoxes.

The question is this: Are there rights, can there be rights, if conditions are such that there is no point in meaningfully asserting them? Granted that we do not have to assert a right in order to have it, can we still be said to have it if there is no *possibility* of our asserting it with a point, i.e., exercising and enjoying it?*

The question is not nonsensical. It compels us to examine more closely the argument that the theoretical case for rights is not affected by a consideration of the conditions of a man's exercising his rights, it being concerned primarily with the conditions of his possessing them. This argument is based on the assumption that we can separate the conditions and determine or define one set apart from the other. I do not think this can be done, especially if we are to explain what it means to have a right.

It would require a great deal to specify correctly the relation between the conditions of having and the conditions of meaningfully asserting and exercising, or, put another way, between the moral power of a claim and the actual power evinced in the exercise of a right, but I think the effort has to be made for a full understanding of the nature of rights. This is not to say that the relation is a logical one. It is true that "I have a right to X" does not *always* imply that I can exercise this right. But there may be a nonlogical sense of "implies" in which it is true to say that having a right implies the possibility of its exercise or assertion with a point.[18]

This amounts to saying that the existence of rights is determined (not necessarily justified) by the complex conditions which render their assertion and exercise possible. The position is not altogether unrelated to that urged by A. I. Melden, who argues that rights-utterances require certain significance conditions if they are to be meaningfully employed.[19]

How would we go about trying to specify the relation between the conditions of having and the conditions of asserting and exercising rights? There are several possible approaches. We could proceed as sociologists and apply empirical tests to determine whether in fact individuals have rights in a given community. Having established this, we could then note how

---

*While "asserting" and "exercising" do not mean the same thing, I am merging them here because it seems to me that when one asserts a right meaningfully or with a point one in doing so in order to either exercise the right or present grounds for doing so.

the conditions of asserting and enjoying bear upon those of possessing rights. But empirical tests are not adequate to determine whether one *has* a right. "I have a right to . . ." or "He a right of . . ." are complex locutions and not always or merely descriptive. One could, as another approach, examine the contexts in which such locutions are uttered and what is understood by them. This is a roundabout method and it may be objected that in employing it one evades the problem. For to note when people talk about their rights is not necessarily to say anything about whether having a right presupposes some conditions under which it may be asserted or enjoyed. But I think the approach can offer some clues. When does a person claim he has a right—not assert, but claim? Is it not usually in circumstances where he feels something can be done to meet his demand?

The expression "I have a right to . . ." can mean a number of things depending on the context in which it is uttered and on the sort of right that is in question. In general I think the expression can be translated into the following locutions at least: "I need X," "I ought to have X," "X is due or owed to me," "I expect X," "I am entitled to X," "I am free to seek X" and "You may not interfere with my getting or doing X." Usually in circumstances where one feels threatened in any way in the securing of an X, or where there is a risk of being deprived, one talks about his right. These are not the only relevant circumstances, for one may also wish to gain something one has not had heretofore, and given the appropriate conditions can claim a right. What, however, characterizes all the circumstances which occasion the talk of rights is an urgent demand that certain objects or services be provided. What do I mean by "talk" here? I mean that whenever anyone says he has a right, whether or not he asserts it, he is implying that he can demand or insist upon certain things. If there is a right, the demand makes sense; but, conversely, it is only when the demanding can make any sense, i.e., can pragmatically be met, that there is a right.

"Pragmatically" is a loaded term. But the idea here is not recondite. John Plamenatz once wrote that a man cannot have the right to move mountains without the aid of tools and this because there does not exist anyone with an obligation correlative to this right.[20] I would say that given the human condition, given the fact that men are not fairy-tale giants and have limited physical strength, such a demand makes no sense. Unless there are relevant mutations within the human race, this demand cannot be met and hence there is no right. This is a gross example, of course, and there are serious problems involved in deciding which demands can or cannot be met pragmatically. We have to appeal to various factors which as was noted earlier are related to the existence of rights, factors such as the rules men obey, available resources, and social ideals.

I seem to be saying that the only rights there are, are the "real" or "actual" rights within a community. Surely there is a difference between having a right and enjoying it? I may have a right which I never in fact exercise for one reason or another. Do I wish to deny this? The answer is no, for what I am saying is that whether a right is merely had or is enjoyed, it is a right—it exists—only to the extent that it *can* be asserted meaningfully, that conditions are such that its exercise is *possible*. There are moral rights, but these too are related to what in fact can be done to realize them, to what is pragmatically possible. Suppose a mythical community where no one thinks there is any point or value to truth-telling. A stranger from another community where truth-telling is valued cannot in this community claim the moral right to be told the truth. His demand makes no sense to persons around him. Indeed, it cannot even be said that he has such a right so long as he remains within this community. Unless there are significant changes in the moral outlook of the natives, he cannot meaningfully claim.

In this particular example it is not so much a matter of what is *pragmatically* possible, for this is primarily a function of communal recognition, available resources, etcetera. We also speak, however, of the ideological or moral contexts which are relevant to or presupposed by rights-discourse. In a community where persons do not acknowledge an obligation to tell the truth or to keep their promises, the relevant moral context which would enable a person to claim the moral right to be told the truth or to have a promise kept is missing. Here, having a right depends upon what is ideologically or morally possible.

It has been suggested that the characteristic function of rights-talk in moral discourse is to provide a moral criticism of interferences with another person's freedom.[21] This interpretation is surely too narrow, even when the discourse is qualified as "moral." As I have suggested, "I have a right to" means more than just "I am justified in doing," or "You are not justified in interfering with. . . ." I would say that this is a minimal meaning or use of the phrase and seems germane to one set of rights, namely, liberties or negative rights to be let alone. The sort of rights which one writer has referred to as "welfare rights," i.e., rights to goods, resources, and services, would seem to require another interpretation.[22] "I have a right to an education" does not mean merely that I can with good moral grounds limit the actions of another person with respect to my demand. It means further, and I would say primarily, that I and others can call upon the active participation and assistance of another person or an institution to provide an education. It means, moreover, that the other person is there and willing to help and that institutions are available or can be provided.

The right to an education, a member of the class of positive *in rem* rights, is peculiar to twentieth-century manifestos. With respect to these rights we cannot easily maintain a distinction between the conditions of having and the conditions of meaningfully asserting. Most human rights belong to this class. Joel Feinberg remarks that these rights do not easily lend themselves to the "schematic translation" in terms of other people's duties because these rights imply more than just dutiful efforts: "Most likely my right in this case . . . entails not simply a duty to try but a responsibility to succeed."[23] If such rights imply responsibilities, they also presuppose conditions under which these responsibilities can be met. If it can be truly said of a person that he has a right to an education or to work or to travel freely, then there must be conditions under which he can assert these rights meaningfully.

It is noted, again by Feinberg, that the sense of "right" implied in the proposed view of what it means for X to have a right to an education is an extended sense of "right," albeit an important and proper one.[24] It is not obvious to me that it is an extended sense. In fact, I would urge that it is the only sense relevant to human rights. It is part of the force of our appeal to a man's human right. Such an appeal amounts to a demand that others—persons or institutions—successfully meet their responsibilities. If they fail, something is terribly wrong, an important commodity is lost.

I have tried in the foregoing discussion to present some considerations in support of a thesis which holds that the possession of a right implies the possibility of its meaningful assertion (where this means not merely saying that one has a right but *standing* on that right) in some nonlogical sense of "implies." Some philosophers admit that this is a reasonable thesis but that it does not amount to much. I have not stated clearly what the other sense of "implies" might be, though my suggestion that the existence of a right depends upon what is pragmatically or ideologically possible within a community is a step in the direction of illuminating this sense. I have wanted mainly to indicate that the relation of entailment, though not a logical one, is nevertheless strong, that the conditions which we take to be relevant to the meaningful assertion of rights cannot wholly be distinguished from those which we regard as relevant to the possession of rights. They are not to be identified either. Their relation has to be specified. The distinction ordinarily drawn between these conditions is not always or even usually reflected in the way we speak about certain rights and what we mean when we claim that a man has a right.

It is probably true, as Salmond wrote a long time ago, that it is not always clear what exactly is being claimed when we say of someone that he has a right.[25] I am recommending that, when we have certain rights in mind, what we mean partially is that the possessor of the right, or others for him, can expect to be able to engage in a number of activities which pertain to his right. I say "partially," for this does not exhaust the meaning of what it is to have a right. But I would argue that this is a basic part of the meaning if not the core. This part has been ignored by those who maintain that there is a clear-cut distinction between the conditions of having and the conditions of meaningfully asserting and exercising a right.

The proposal here is very much in the nature of a program.

There are obvious conceptual difficulties. Given these, one wonders how far such a proposal can go. If we maintain that rights exist not simply wherever there are sentient beings with interests and needs but where, further, a number of conditions obtain which make the meaningful assertion of these rights possible, we appear to discount the talk of rights as claims or possible claims. We ignore the manner in which "having a right" is related to "having a claim" or "being entitled to." And this is plainly an important side of rights. What if conditions are such that it is impossible or very difficult to exercise or enjoy a right? There are societies in underdeveloped countries where resources and institutions are lamentably lacking, and the rights ascribed to the members of these societies by the United Nations Declaration for instance, cannot be meaningfully asserted, or such assertions amount in effect to "voices in the wilderness." It would seem that the proposal requires us to say that these persons do not have rights. And if we do admit this, are we not, in the final analysis, identifying the conditions of having with those of meaningfully asserting and exercising? In this case the proposal cannot explain how rights may be denied and yet continue to be rights.

The view urged here appears to smack too much of a positivistic account of rights, and therefore can hardly be associated with the name of T. H. Green, who argued against the theories of Spinoza, Hobbes, and Austin on this score. But to say that we cannot maintain a clear-cut distinction between the conditions of possessing and those of exercising a right, to urge that there is a vital point of contact between these conditions, is not to equate rights with powers nor to say that rights exist only to the extent that there are sanctions which enforce correlative duties. A possessor of a right need not himself have the power, though, on the view presented here, his right presupposes that something *can* be done—whether or not it is in fact done—to secure what is claimed as a matter of right. Nor is it being maintained that to have a right means to have an assurance. I may, in fact, feel assured that certain things will be done or refrained from which meet my demands, but it is not merely in virtue of my right that I feel this. If the proposal has any recommendation on the matter of what it means to have a right, it is the idea that to have a right is to have grounds for reasonable expectations.

I have noted certain problems here because I think they must be resolved by the thesis if it is to emerge as a useful account of how rights exist and what it means for them to exist. Given the aforementioned difficulties we may wonder about the conceptual advantages of the thesis. It invites many muddles; does it at least illuminate anything? I think it makes us aware, as we ought to be but seldom are, of the fragile nature of rights,[26] especially moral and human rights. Like moral rules these rights are fragile in the sense that their existence depends on so many factors which are obscured when we suppose that there need only be persons for there to be rights. This is an undeniably necessary condition but not a sufficient one. Rights require a great deal. The extent to which we *can* ascribe rights (not ought to) depends upon the communal and ideological-moral environment.

This view alerts us to the fact that much needs to be done in the environment to secure the setting for rights. In one sense, of course, the "setting" is there; there are persons with needs and interests which they can communicate to others; there are ideals and purposive actions of all sorts. There are, further, institutions and rules, but we are not always aware of their function in or for the existence of rights. Yet the existence of rights is not automatic. It is not for nothing that the achievement of rights—not merely the legal variety—has historically been associated with struggle of one kind or another. If we count rights as "important commodities," then we must be vigilant. The existence of rights requires more than just the existence of men. This view suggests that we are not to look upon lists of rights as merely a catalogue of possessions whose removal gives us cause for righteous indignation; we are to take these lists as urgent recommendations for action.

To the question "why rights at all?" one recent writer has urged very simply: "If we are asked, why ought anyone to have a right to anything? or why not have a system in which there are not rights at all? The answer is that such a system would be a morally impoverished one."[27] Green would readily concur, but the matter does not end there. He thought it important to determine the moral purpose rights serve, what, in other words, is the "moral enrichment" in the life of man which rights bring about and which justifies their existence.

His thesis on the common good is an attempt to answer this question. In my reconstruction of this thesis I suggested a possible reading of the principle of the common good as a rights-conferring ideal. In this interpretation the common good emerges as an ideal of equality, justice, and freedom; these are typically the ideals of the moral community. They are also conditions for the realization of human capabilities. It is by appeal to such principles that various rights are determined, and rights are viewed as conditions for self-realization. The moral community is achieved to the extent that human beings develop certain attributes and capacities which enable them to foster and sustain an "ever-widening social union." Human rights in this analysis turn out to be conditions for the development of a moral community among men, and this is the good which is common to all men.

A number of objections have been brought against the procedure of equating the ideals or principles of equality, justice, and freedom, and that of the common good. There is the argument that lumping these distinct concepts together simply ignores the specific function which each performs in our moral and political thinking.[28] We frequently appeal to one principle to justify a specific course of action which on another principle would not be justified. Philosophers who argue in this way are usually quick to point out that promoting the common good sometimes involves bypassing the requirements of equality, justice, and freedom, for on this view the common good is primarily the "result" of various methods of aggregation, whereas concepts like justice and equality indicate distributive comparisons.[29] Extending this argument to a theory of rights, one could say that the rights which are justified by considerations of social justice or the principle of equal freedom are not always the rights allowed by the principle of the common good and may indeed clash with the latter.

Another objection is aimed specifically at the equation between justice and the common good. It is urged that justice is not the whole of morality—that "just-making considerations are only one species of right-making considerations."[30] To equate justice with the common good is to erase the boundary between it and moral goodness or rightness. In this view the common good is a principle of morality, and it is not certain that rights derive from right-making considerations. Hart has argued that the sort of considerations which are relevant to establishing that one has or ought to have a right (he considers one right in his discussion, the equal right of all men to be free) are quite different from those which are pertinent to justifying a duty. He urges a bifurcation of morality into two spheres, one being the sphere to which rights belong, the other the sphere of duties.[31] The moral justification offered for rights involves appeal to a principle of equal freedom, whereas we justify duties by appealing to various principles such as utility, beneficence, etcetera. It follows from this, according to Hart, that having a right and benefiting from a duty performed cannot be identified. He who has a right does not always stand to benefit by the performance of an obligation correlative to his right. It is therefore not correct to say that standing to benefit by such a performance establishes that one has a right. But on the theory that the common good justifies rights, some sort of identification appears to be drawn between having a right and benefiting by the performance of a duty. Does not Green maintain in effect that the degree to which one stands to benefit justifies us in ascribing a right to that person? He does appear to think that benefiting in some sense, whether by the performance of a duty or something else, is intimately connected with having rights, and that this fact figures importantly in our justification of rights.

The extent to which Green equates various principles is debatable. I would say that he does not so much *equate* the principles of justice, equality, freedom, and the common good. His point is that the common good is achieved to the degree that the ideals of justice and the rest are pursued and abided by. In his theory there is no tension between these ideals, but he does admit that the rules and considerations of justice, for instance, are determined independently of a theory of the *summum bonum*. This does not mean, of course, that they cannot be employed to define and achieve the latter.

There is a labyrinth of issues here, and the scope of this book does not permit an examination of these in any detail. Perhaps in treating the common good as a rights-conferring

ideal—in urging that all rights are directly or indirectly relative to a common good—Green has put too many eggs in one
basket. One writer who maintains that the principle of the
common good is concerned with rights notes that it is relevant
to "positive 'passive' rights" while the principle of equal freedom is concerned with "negative 'passive' rights."[32] The point
is that different principles are employed to justify different
rights. Has Green a conception in mind so wide as to render it
vacuous? If this is the case we cannot decide on the basis of
his conception of the common good why a system with rights
is preferable to one without, nor which rights are to be allowed and whether these are absolute in some sense.

I do not think it is a vacuous conception but I shall not
argue this point further..I have tried to render this conception meaningful in my reconstruction. I shall concentrate
here on certain aspects of Green's justification of rights. Specifically, I ask whether the principle of the common good in the
theory of rights is primarily a principle of morality—whether,
that is, Green justifies rights by maintaining that they are
conditions for right conduct. I shall focus on the following issues in an attempt to answer this question: first, the issue of
the relation between having a right and "being required"; second, the matter of whether or not exercising a right is acting
rightly in some sense; and third, the issue of the waivability of
rights. I shall discuss these matters not in any particular order
but all together, for they are all related to the main question
of whether there is some important connection between rights
(having and exercising) and right conduct such that one can
justify the former in terms of the latter.

Let us first of all recall some of the statements Green employs when he undertakes to justify rights or to answer the
question "why rights at all?" He says that rights are necessary
to a man's acting as a moral person at all (29LP), that they are
important for the development of a "moral capacity without
which a man would not be a man" (30LP), that they are required by the "consciousness that the common good should be
the object of action, i.e., a duty." (30LP)

Everything hinges on how we interpret "moral capacity"
and "acting as a moral person." As I have been maintaining, I
do not think Green is saying that rights are necessary for the

performance of duties. They are necessary for the realization of certain capacities which include, but are not to be equated with, the capacities to perform duties. The point is: it is not because they are capacities to perform duties that they ought to be realized and that there should be rights; it is that they ought to be realized because they are *human* capacities, capacities for all sorts of things including the performance of duties, human fellowship, artistic and intellectual work, family living, generosity, etcetera; in short, capacities for realizing the stuff of which the good life is made, without which a man would not be a man.

But there is the term "moral"; it crops up everywhere in Green's work. In the theory of rights the term has a special meaning. It does not mean "conscientiousness" merely. The force of the term is in the first place to indicate that not all human capacities are to be realized as a matter of right. We cannot claim the right to perpetrate the evil of which man is capable. Second, "moral" implies "purposive." Third, it implies "urgent for the self."

In a challenging article W. D. Falk offers some grounds for regarding merely personal oughts as having the importance and urgency of social oughts, which are usually considered *moral* oughts proper.[33] On this argument the term "moral" ought not to be restricted to those actions and desires which affect and benefit other people; it can be assigned also to those demands which one makes on oneself which are treated normally as merely prudential but which in fact are urgent and important enough to the individual to be considered moral. They are moral because when an individual fails to meet and satisfy these demands which he makes on himself, there is cause for self-reproach. Such a demand as "I ought to save money because I want to provide a college education for my children" is, according to Falk's thesis, a moral ought.

Green too employs "moral" in this sense, that is, to characterize those demands which an individual makes on himself, which have "special force and urgency." These demands and the capacities to meet them are what make a man a man. A person claims and can claim rights to satisfy these demands.

This is part of the wide sense of "moral" which figures in the theory of rights and for which Green was indebted to the philosophies of Plato and Aristotle. The Greek notion *to oikeion*, translated loosely as *belonging* to one or as *suitable* for one, can be employed to elucidate the conception of self-realization as a moral end, though I shall not attempt to do so here.[34] I suggest simply that "moral" for Green has the further connotation of "suitable" or "fitting." The demands which we make on ourselves which we claim rights to meet, as well as the desires we seek to satisfy which are relevant to our rights-claims, are part of the total picture of what is suitable or fitting for us.[35] We do not always seek *to oikeion*. Hence the relevance of the ought in this context.

But, and this is important to remember, the moral end for Green is both a personal and a social ideal. My commitment to the demands I make on myself is a commitment to others. What I ought to do for myself does not differ except in special content from what I ought to do for others. Thus the end is described as a common good.

Rights, then, are related to and required by a moral end which is construed widely as a set of projected personal ideals as well as a social requirement. Even in this wide sense it appears to follow, first, that wherever a right is claimed or asserted, something is required; second, since the right is justified by reference to a moral end, whether personal or social, exercising that right *is* acting rightly; and third, it does not make sense to say that rights ought to be waived in certain circumstances. These follow because where we want to say that rights are relative to a moral end we are in effect asserting that rights are conditions for right conduct in some sense of "right." And if we do maintain this, are we not confusing matters and misconstruing the nature of rights?

An important argument has been urged against the procedure of deriving the rights a person has from considerations of what it is right to do, whether one is doing right by oneself or others. Let us review this argument briefly and then consider whether it can apply to the rights Green is discussing, namely, "natural," or human, rights.

According to Abraham Melden, some philosophers, and he cites Bradley, Maritain, and Ewing, confuse two quite distinct notions, obligation-meeting action and obligatory action.[36] This results in their treating locutions about rights as though they were locutions about what it is right do do, or right conduct. They have thus overlooked the important fact that what is correlative to a right is obligation-meeting action, not obligatory action, and where an action is obligation-meeting it is not necessarily obligatory. Melden argues for this distinction by noting that there are circumstances where standing on one's right—making an issue of "one's privileged moral position"—is ill-advised and morally unjustified. In such cases exercising a right is not necessarily acting rightly; in fact, it may be morally desirable to waive one's right in these circumstances, and we would not want to say that in doing so one was ner and action of a boor or a pharisee to stand on a right. It may be morally offensive. In circumstances where what is at stake is a trifling matter, it is, according to Melden, the manner and action of a boor or a pharisee to stand on a right. It may be morally desirable to waive one's right in these circumstances, and we would not want to say that in doing so one was guilty of a failure in "moral nerve." It is not self-contradictory to say that one is or can be morally justified in waiving one's moral right. Exercising a right is fundamentally different from performing a duty or acting rightly (though Melden also maintains that they are related in some way). In the view that rights are conditions for right conduct or are required by considerations of what is good for the possessor of the right as well as for others against whom the right exists, it is impossible to account for waivability or for the fact that moral rights compete for satisfaction.

Melden's argument is an important one. Few philosophers would want to argue that there are no circumstances where one is justified in waiving a right. But Melden is able to advance his case neatly because he has in mind certain special moral rights, such as the right of a parent to special consideration. It seems to me that the strength of his argument rests partially on his reference to "trifling matters." We are not morally justified in asserting a right where the matter is of slight importance. Of course, our waiving of a right might be justified by certain overriding moral considerations. In these circumstances asserting a right or attempting to exercise it is morally wrong. Melden cites examples where a parent would be acting wrongly if he stood on his right to special considerations, thus interfering with his son's obligation to keep a promise to a friend or with his son's right to study.

But does the argument easily hold up when we consider human rights? In what sort of circumstances is one ill-advised and *morally* unjustified in standing on one's human right? We are all too ready to admit these circumstances, but in fact we rarely say what they are. Are there any? One may not in fact be able to stand on such a right (i.e., meaningfully assert it) because there is a scarcity of resources, a lack of communal aid, recognition, etcetera, but when is one not *justified* in asserting such a right? Human rights usually have to do with things that are important; what is at stake is not normally a trifling matter.

I think human rights present a special problem for "waivability." I do not wish to deny that such rights compete for satisfaction, but I think it is difficult and perhaps even dangerous to maintain that the reasons for this competition are moral ones. In the case of a parent and his son the moral rights and obligations of each may compete on moral grounds. Consider, however, X's human right to an education or adequate medical care. This may compete with Y's human right to freedom of movement where Y happens to be a doctor or a teacher. The demands of both X and Y are serious, equally urgent and worthwhile; no trifling matter is at stake. Is either morally justified in waiving his right? Is it not more correct to say that one or the other is *compelled* under the circumstances to waive his right? It is not as if the demands of one take *moral* precedence over those of the other; the competition does not derive from the moral superiority or urgency of one human right over the other. It derives from the fact that both rights cannot be exercised at the same time for *pragmatic*, not moral reasons.

It seems to be a special fact about human rights, however they are justified, that each one is important and fundamental. We are often compelled to waive a human right, but this is lamentable and not easily morally justified. With respect to such rights we feel it is imperative that conditions be secured so that competition between them is minimal. The well-being of every human being depends upon this.

It may be countered that insofar as human rights are a

species of moral rights they too are subject to the tensions and conflicts which exist between the latter. This may be granted. What I am querying is whether the competition arises from a conflict between moral rules and principles or from the fact that a scarcity of resources of all sorts makes it difficult to meet the demands expressed by various human rights. If a human right is waived, it is usually because its possessor cannot do otherwise. One rarely pats oneself on the back for doing so, as a parent might when he waives his right to special consideration, unless one happens to be a saint or a hero. But then, saints and heroes do not normally worry about their *rights;* the language and the concepts they employ go beyond the special discourse about rights and duties.

There is an important connection between allowing certain rights as human and what we take to be "right" for men in general. If we do not construe "right conduct" in a narrow sense, this connection is clear. And it is because we think that these rights are crucial commodities for the sort of activities which comprise the good life that we balk at the idea of having to waive them in certain circumstances, in a way in which we are not so troubled by having to waive a special moral right.

It does seem that in the case of a human right, acting so as to exercise the right is acting rightly, though it does not follow from this that failure so to act is a failure in "moral nerve." What compels us to assert a right is a function of many factors and not simply the desire to do right by ourselves or others. The point is that a supporter of the thesis that rights are justified by considerations of right conduct need not maintain that one must always assert one's rights, for the latter are not the only means available to one for acting rightly.

Those who deny that there is this intimate connection between having a human right and acting rightly often appeal, as I have noted, to special rights to support their argument. Thus, Joel Feinberg remarks that when one votes for a candidate for public office one is exercising a right, but this does not mean he has acted rightly because he may not have voted for the right candidate. He admits that even in this case it may be true to say that the person has acted rightly in voting at all, and so he appeals to a counterexample, to wit, Shylock's right to a pound of flesh which is, of course, a special right created by contract.[37]

But human rights are not like Shylock's right to a pound of flesh. In the case of the former even Portia may not appeal to mercy to temper the requirements of justice. Can one be criticized for exercising a human right?

This question can be answered only by deciding what sort of ideal—social or moral—is relevant to human rights and therefore what rights are to count as human rights. Whatever the ideal, however, it remains true that one cannot easily divorce "having a human right" from "acting rightly." Those who accept this, however, do not go on to subscribe to the further contention that considerations of right conduct are relevant to justifying human rights in general. And this because, it is argued, exercising the latter does not always mean acting rightly.

Take the right to free speech. Is it true that exercising this right is acting "in a way that gives appreciable assurance of immunity from criticism"?[38] Suppose one delivers speeches intended to undermine the institutions which foster the rights of man? Surely one may be *criticized* for doing so, though not punished.[39] But here again, what is our objection? Are we criticizing a member of the John Birch Society for speaking freely or are we taking issue with the content of his speech? I would suggest the latter. It is one thing to take a man to task for saying what is on his mind, quite another to disagree with what he is saying. We may not do the former but we can certainly do the latter. A John Bircher is acting rightly when he exercises his right—in Hart's terms his action ensures the distribution of freedom and this is right—though we may not in fact think that what he is saying is true, right, etcetera.

It is often urged that there is an essential contrast between having a right and "being required."[40] I do not see that this contrast is essential or obvious. I may not be required to seek an education because I have a right to an education; it is not always true that a right is a ground for a duty. This much is granted. But may I not say that my having such a right derives in part from my having made this a requirement for what I consider the good life? It is true that having a right and being required are not the same, but neither is there an essential contrast between them. Those who link locutions about rights to locutions about right conduct are not committed to saying that one has a right whenever one is required to do something. Having a right may not be relevant at all to fulfilling a requirement or doing what is required. They are saying that certain requirements which one has set for oneself and for others are grounds for certain rights.

Insofar as Green does not maintain that rights are conditions for conscientious action or for adherence to a Kantian moral law, he is not guilty of a certain type of confusion between locutions about rights and those of right conduct. But he does seem to think that we cannot wholly determine what rights ought to be allowed apart from considerations of what it is right to do either for oneself or for others. In the preceding discussion I have tried to focus on certain aspects of human rights which suggest that we cannot easily deny the intimate connection between rights and right conduct construed widely, and that in justifying human rights we do appeal to principles or ideals which have the urgency and cogency of moral principles even if they are not exactly the same as the latter.

Much, however, needs to be done to establish this thesis, and my remarks so far have been "feelers" in this direction. Most of its proponents assume it to be true without further argument. Yet there are questions and problems.

How are we to define "right conduct" so that the relation between it and having or exercising rights is not trivialized or misleading? If we want to maintain that the ideal which justifies and confers rights is such as to make it difficult to account for, i.e., justify, the waiving of a human right, then what happens to the time-honored thesis that all rights are at most *prima facie*? Does a proponent of the view examined here maintain that there are no conditions under which human rights may properly be overridden? Is one not committed to saying that these rights are absolute when one urges that waivability of a human right is not *morally* justified? Implicit in the view urged here is the idea that the exercise of a human right is always desirable.

Actually it does not follow from "exercising a human right is acting rightly" that there are no circumstances under which a right may be overridden. The case most often cited to show that rights are not absolute is that of the criminal. We are justified, we feel, in placing constraints on the criminal's freedom of movement. What is not often noted in this matter is that it was not in the exercise of any right that the criminal acted wrongly. If he stole, murdered, or did anything that is in the nature of a criminal act, he did not do these in the exercise of his right to freedom, for the latter does not confer any additional rights to act criminally. We say that by his actions he *forfeited* his right to freedom of movement. If it is possible to forfeit a right, then there are circumstances when a right may be properly overridden.

But the problem remains. We want to be able to say that a right may be overridden in consequence of the fact that it is being misused or that there are more important considerations than the right itself. It would seem that this view does not allow us to say this easily. I do not think a proponent of the view has to say that rights are absolute. What is being urged is that we are to consider circumstances which compel the overriding of a human right as unfortunate because something precious is being lost. The moral resolution achieved in the "justified" overriding of such a right is purchased at a heavy price, and we lose sight of this fact when we consider rights of all sorts as merely *prima facie*.

Notes and References

Chapter 1

1. James Bryce, *Studies in Contemporary Biography* (London, 1903), p. 99.
2. P. H. Partridge, "Politics, Philosophy, Ideology," rpt. in Anthony Quinton, ed., *Political Philosophy* (Oxford, 1968), p. 34.
3. For contemporary critical reviews of the notion of the common good, see various essays in Carl Friedrich, ed., *The Public Interest*, Nomos V. (New York, 1962).
4. Melvin Richter, *The Politics of Conscience: T. H. Green and His Age* (Boston, 1964), pp. 222-23.
5. George H. Sabine, *A History of Political Theory* (New York, 1945), p. 677.

Chapter 2

1. Quoted by Richter in *The Politics of Conscience*, p. 56.
2. *Ibid.*, p. 42.
3. R. C. K. Ensor, *England: 1870-1914* (Oxford, 1936), p. 162.
4. Quoted by Richter, p. 153.
5. *Ibid.*
6. F. H. Bradley, *Essays on Truth and Reality* (Oxford, 1914), p. 15.
7. In a letter from J. A. Symonds to Green's wife, quoted by Richter, p. 163n.
8. Quoted by Richter, pp. 82-83.
9. From Lord Asquith's *Memoirs,* quoted by Richter, p. 162.
10. Henry Sidgwick, *The Ethics of T. H. Green, Mr. Herbert Spencer and J. Martineau* (London, 1902), pp. 80-99.
11. Richter, p. 341.
12. Quoted by Richter, p. 94.
13. *Ibid.*, p. 109.
14. Letter from Green to Holland, December 29, 1868, quoted by Richter, p. 30.
15. Letter from Green to Holland, January 6, 1869, quoted by Richter, pp. 31-32.
16. Richter, p. 134.
17. Letter from Green to Holland, quoted by Richter, p. 117.

18. *Ibid.*
19. Quoted by Richter, p. 137.

Chapter 3

1. C. A. Campbell, "Moral Intuition and the Principle of Self-Realization," rpt. in *In Defense of Free Will* (London and New York, 1967), p. 127.
2. A. MacBeath, *Experiments in Living* (London, 1958), p. 412.
3. Campbell, p. 127.
4. Ibid., p. 133.
5. Henry Sidgwick, *Lectures on the Ethics of T. H. Green, Mr. Herbert Spencer and J. Martineau* (London, 1902), p. 71.
6. H. D. Lewis, "Does the Good Will Define its Own Content?" rpt. in *Freedom and History* (London, 1962), p. 13.

Chapter 4

1. Cf. L. T. Hobhouse, *The Elements of Social Justice* (London, 1965), p. 39.
2. H. A. Prichard, *Moral Obligation* (Oxford, 1949), p. 58.
3. Green's argument is not unlike that of Hart, who has urged that the concepts of a right and an obligation are among those moral concepts whose most important characteristic is that "there is no incongruity, but a special congruity in the use of force or the threat of force to secure that what is . . . someone's right to have done shall in fact be done." H. L. A. Hart, "Are There Any Natural Rights?" *The Philosophical Review*, 64 (1955), 178. Hart, like Green, bases his argument on a distinction advanced by Kant between duties as *officia juris* (what Green and Hart call "obligations") and duties as *officia virtutis*. See Kant, *The Metaphysical Elements of Justice*, tr. John Ladd (Indianapolis, 1965), p. 45.
4. Green is not entirely fair to Locke, for the latter does not divorce rights from operative social rules but only from enforced laws. See Hobhouse, p. 35.
5. W. D. Lamont, *Introduction to Green's Moral Philosophy* (London, 1934), p. 212.
6. Hart, p. 175.
7. See W. K. Frankena, "Symposium: The Concept of Universal Human Rights," *Science, Language and Human Rights* (Philadelphia, 1952), p. 201.
8. A. I. Melden, *Rights and Right Conduct* (Oxford, 1959), p. 61.
9. Margaret Macdonald, "Natural Rights," rpt. in Peter Laslett, ed., *Philosophy, Politics and Society* (Oxford, 1963), p. 47.

10. See Dorothy Emmet, *Function, Purpose and Powers* (London, 1958), p. 22.

11. John Plamenatz, *Consent, Freedom and Political Obligation*, 2nd. ed. (1938; rpt. New York, 1968), pp. 87-88.

12. The phrase "regular and intimate" is taken from Plamenatz, p. 87.

Chapter 5

1. See E. F. Carritt, *Ethical and Political Thinking* (Oxford, 1947), p. 154, and A. C. Ewing, *The Individual, the State and World Government* (New York, 1947), pp. 22-28.

2. See Joel Feinberg, "Duties, Rights, and Claims," *American Philosophical Quarterly*, 3, No. 2 (April, 1966), 142; and Martin Golding, "Towards a Theory of Human Rights," *The Monist*, 4, (1968).

3. Frankena, "Symposium: The Concept of Universal Human Rights," p. 201.

4. Cf. H. L. A. Hart, "The Ascription of Responsibility and Rights," rpt. in Antony Flew, ed., *Logic and Language* (New York, 1965), p. 151.

5. Ewing, p. 22.

6. *Ibid.*, p. 23.

7. W. D. Ross, *The Right and the Good* (Oxford, 1955), p. 51.

8. Plamenatz, *Consent, Freedom and Political Obligation*, pp. 90-91.

9. Hobhouse, *The Elements of Social Justice*, p. 43.

10. Bernard Bosanquet, *The Philosophical Theory of the State* (London, 1899), p. 196.

11. *Ibid.*, p. 197.

12. Ross, p. 51.

13. H. D. Lewis, "Individualism and Collectivism," in *Freedom and History*, p. 87.

14. *Ibid.*, pp. 87-88.

15. Ross, p. 51.

16. Macdonald, "Natural Rights," p. 50.

17. Lewis, p. 80.

18. Plamenatz, p. 94.

19. See Golding, p. 529 and passim.

20. Plamenatz, p. 99.

Chapter 6

1. Brian Barry, *Political Argument* (London, 1968), p. 204.

2. Lewis, "Individualism and Collectivism" in *Freedom and History*, pp. 61-62.

3. *Ibid.,* p. 63.

4. Green's list of fundamental rights (the sense of "fundamental" is discussed in a later chapter) nowhere approaches the complexity of the United Nations Declaration. He does not, for instance, talk about various welfare rights, though what he says about rights in general can accommodate the rights which have come to be regarded as crucial. See Green, "Liberal Legislation and Freedom of Contract," *Works,* III, pp. 365-386.

5. See Barry for a very thorough analysis of how such concepts are ordinarily employed. Also see Alan Gewirth, "Political Justice," in Richard Brandt, ed., *Social Justice* (Englewood Cliffs, N. J., 1962), pp. 162-69.

6. L. T. Hobhouse, *Liberalism* (New York, 1964), p. 68.

7. Macdonald, "Natural Rights," p. 48.

8. David Ritchie, *Natural Rights* (London, 1952), p. 101.

9. J. G. Hobson, *The Social Problem,* quoted by Hobhouse, *The Elements of Social Justice,* p. 43.

10. I have been inspired to think along these lines by my reading of Barry. While I disagree with his interpretation of both Green and Hobhouse, I have found his critical analysis of certain issues invaluable.

11. Green considered it important for the existence of rights that the ideal in reference to which a claim is made be *acknowledged* by those who make and concede claims. What this *acknowledgment* of a common good amounts to is a question I consider in the following chapter.

12. Barry, 230-32.

13. Hobhouse was influenced by Green, but this may not be sufficient ground for applying criticism aimed at one theory to another. In this case, however, I think it can be done, for Hobhouse acknowledges his debt to Green. See Hobhouse, *Liberalism,* pp. 67-69.

14. Barry, p. 311.

15. *Ibid.,* p. 231.

16. Richter, *The Politics of Conscience,* p. 257.

17. The editor of the *Prolegomena,* A. C. Bradley, offers a possible answer which is consonant with the major contentions of that work. See Green, *Prolegomena,* p. 344n.

Chapter 7

1. Cf. Richter, *The Politics of Conscience,* p. 229.

2. Cf. H. D. Lewis, "T. H. Green and Rousseau," in *Freedom and History,* pp. 106-133.

3. A. J. M. Milne, *The Social Philosophy of English Idealism* (London, 1962), p. 129.

4. Cf. S. I. Benn and R. S. Peters, *The Principles of Political Thought* (New York, 1965), pp. 318-21.

5. Plamenatz, *Consent, Freedom and Political Obligation,* pp. 62-81.

6. *Ibid.,* p. 72.

7. Gewirth, "Political Justice," pp. 158-59.

8. *Ibid.*

9. *Ibid.*

10. Lamont, *Introduction to Green's Moral Philosophy,* p. 216.

11. *Ibid.,* p. 217.

12. Sidgwick, *Lectures on the Ethics of T. H. Green,* pp. 1-99.

13. *Ibid.,* p. 69.

14. *Ibid.,* pp. 66-67.

15. *Ibid.,* p. 64.

16. *Nicomachean Ethics,* Book VIII, 1155a, 25-26.

17. C. B. Macpherson, "The Maximization of Democracy," rpt. in Laslett and Runciman, eds., *Philosophy, Politics and Society,* Third Series (Oxford, 1967), p. 101.

18. *Ibid.*

19. A problem which Green does not consider is the extent to which the common good is undermined by *real* scarcity as opposed to an ideology of scarcity.

20. See A. I. Melden, "Symposium: The Concept of Universal Human Rights," in *Science, Language and Human Rights* (Philadelphia, 1952), p. 186.

21. See H. D. Lewis, "Does the Good Will Define its Own Content?" in *Freedom and History,* p. 22.

22. On Green's supposed failure to distinguish between "locutions about rights" and "locutions about what it is right to do," see my comments in chapter eight, where I discuss some problems in Green's view.

23. Prichard, *Moral Obligation,* p. 79.

Chapter 8

1. Prichard, *Moral Obligation,* pp. 54ff.

2. A. I. Melden, *Rights and Right Conduct,* p. 1.

3. He limits rights to persons in the sense that he denies that animals have rights. His argument on this matter is not very cogent. He maintains that we cannot endow animals with rights because we cannot attribute to them a conscious interest in a common good. In their behavior animals are never affected or motivated by concep-

tions of an ideal. It does not make sense, therefore, to talk about their rights. (208LP) Now, we may argue against Green that we cannot decide whether or not animals have "conceptions"; our lines of communication with them do not meet on an abstract level. But this is not to say that we cannot detect "motivation" in animals. Surely animals have goals in some sense. If Green wants to maintain only that the goals of an animal and those of a human being do not ever coincide in what can be called a common good, he still does not have a case; for we cannot deny that some, at least, of the needs and efforts of quadrupeds are shared by human beings, e.g., the desire to be relieved from pain, to be fed, to move about freely, to rest. Finally, animals *are* capable of some sort of fellowship with human beings—as the adage has it, "A dog is man's best friend," etc. Are not these considerations for endowing animals with rights?

4. Macdonald, "Natural Rights," p. 44.

5. See P. F. Strawson, "Social Morality and Individual Ideal," *Philosophy,* XXXVI (January, 1961), 1-17.

6. Shils is quoted by Partridge in "Politics, Philosophy, Ideology," p. 41.

7. See Golding, "Towards a Theory of Human Rights," pp. 524-25.

8. H. L. A. Hart, *The Concept of Law* (Oxford, 1961), pp. 190-93.

9. *Ibid.,* p. 193.

10. See W. D. Lamont, *Principles of Moral Judgement* (Oxford, 1946), pp. 124-29. Lamont bases his discussion on cases in English and Scottish law.

11. *Ibid.,* p. 127.

12. H. D. Lewis, "Individualism and Collectivism," in *Freedom and History,* pp. 84-85.

13. See Richard Wasserstrom, "Rights, Human Rights and Racial Discrimination," *Journal of Philosophy,* LXI, 20 (October 29, 1964), 633n.

14. See Lamont, p. 79, for the definition of rights as powers given by Gray and Vinogradoff.

15. *Ibid.,* p. 78.

16. See S. M. Brown, Jr., "Inalienable Rights," *The Philosophical Review,* 64 (1955), 200-203.

17. Brown, pp. 203-204, remarks correctly that it is important to assert rights, for this is a condition for political and social justice.

18. Cf. W. K. Frankena, "Natural and Inalienable Rights," *The Philosophical Review,* 64 (1955), 226-27. Frankena makes this point, but seems to think it is a weak claim. On the other hand, Brown, p. 200, writes: "In order for there to be rights, there must be some conditions under which they can be meaningfully asserted."

19. Melden, "Symposium: The Concept of Universal Human Rights," *Science, Language and Human Rights* (Philadelphia, 1952), pp. 167-87.

20. Plamenatz, *Consent, Freedom and Political Obligation,* pp. 82-83.

21. Hart, "Are There Any Natural Rights?," p. 189.

22. Golding, "Towards a Theory of Human Rights," p. 542.

23. Feinberg, "Duties, Rights, and Claims," p. 143.

24. *Ibid.*

25. *Salmond on Jurisprudence,* P. J. Fitzgerald, ed., 12th ed. (London, 1966), p. 217.

26. I have borrowed the term "fragile" from Golding.

27. Wasserstrom, p. 636.

28. See Brian Barry, "Justice and the Common Good," rpt. in Anthony Quinton, ed., *Political Philosophy* (Oxford, 1967), pp. 189-93.

29. *Ibid.*

30. W. K. Frankena, "The Concept of Social Justice," in Richard Brandt, ed., *Social Justice* (Englewood Cliffs, N. J.: 1962), p. 5.

31. Hart, "Are There Any Natural Rights?" pp. 177-78ff.

32. Gewirth, "Political Justice," p. 156.

33. W. D. Falk, "Morality, Self and Others," rpt. in Castaneda and Nakhnikian, eds., *Morality and the Language of Conduct* (Detroit, 1963), pp. 25-47.

34. See Ann R. Cacoullos, *Plato's Theory of Love,* unpublished M.A. Thesis, Columbia, 1962.

35. Cf. Frankena, "Natural and Inalienable Rights," pp. 226-27.

36. Melden, *Rights and Right Conduct,* pp. 9-20.

37. Feinberg, "Wasserstrom on Human Rights," *Journal of Philosophy,* LXI, 20 (October 29, 1964), 642-43.

38. Wasserstrom, p. 630.

39. See Feinberg, p. 643.

40. *Ibid.*

Selected Bibliography

PRIMARY SOURCES

GREEN, THOMAS HILL. *Works*. Ed. R. L. Nettleship. 3 Vols. London: Longmans, 1885-88.
———. *Prolegomena to Ethics*. Ed. A. C. Bradley. Oxford: Clarendon, 1883.
———. *Lectures on the Principles of Political Obligation*. Rpt. London: Longmans, 1963, and Michigan: Ann Arbor Paperbacks, 1967.

SECONDARY SOURCES

1. Biographical
NETTLESHIP, R. L. *Memoir of Thomas Hill Green*. London: Longmans, 1906.
RICHTER, MELVIN. *The Politics of Conscience: T. H. Green and His Times*. Boston: Harvard University Press, 1964.

2. On Green's Moral Philosophy
FAIRBROTHER, W. H. *The Philosophy of Thomas Hill Green*. London: Methuen, 1896.
CAMPBELL, A. C. "Moral Intuition and the Principle of Self-Realization." *In Defense of Free-Will*. London: Allen and Unwin, 1967.
LAMONT, W. D. *Introduction to Green's Moral Philosophy*. London: George Allen and Unwin, 1934.
LEWIS, H. D. "Does the Good Will Define its Own Content?" *Freedom and History*. London: George Allen and Unwin, 1962.
SIDGWICK, HENRY. *Lectures on the Ethics of T. H. Green, Mr. Herbert Spencer and J. Martineau*. London, 1902.

3. On Green's Political Theory
BARKER, ERNEST. *Political Thought in England 1848 to 1914*. London: Oxford University Press, 1954.
CHIN, Y. ,. *The Political Theory of Thomas Hill Green*. New York: W. D. Gray, 1920.

LEWIS, H. D. "Individualism and Collectivism: A Study of Thomas Hill Green." *Freedom and History*. London: George Allen and Unwin, 1962.

MACCUNN, JOHN. *Six Radical Thinkers*. Rpt. New York, 1964.

MILNE, A. J. M. *The Social Philosophy of English Idealism*. London: George Allen and Unwin, 1962.

MUIRHEAD, J. H. *The Service of the State*. London, 1908.

PLAMENATZ, JOHN. *Consent, Freedom and Political Obligation*. 2nd. ed. New York: Oxford, 1968.

PRICHARD, H. A. "Green's Principles of Political Obligation." *Moral Obligation*. Oxford: Clarendon, 1949.

4. In the Tradition of Green's Political Theory

BOSANQUET, BERNARD. *The Philosophical Theory of the State*. London, 1899.

HOBHOUSE, L. T. *The Elements of Social Justice*. Rpt. London: George Allen and Unwin, 1965.

————. *The Rational Good*. London: George Allen and Unwin, 1921.

————. *Liberalism*. Rpt. New York: Oxford, 1964.

RITCHIE, DAVID. *Natural Rights*. London, 1894.

5. Contemporary Works on Rights and Related Issues

BARRY, BRIAN. *Political Argument*. New York: Humanities Press, 1968.

BENN, S. I., and R. S. PETERS. *The Principles of Political Thought*. New York: Free Press, 1965.

BERLIN, SIR ISAIAH. *Two Concepts of Liberty*. Oxford: Clarendon, 1958.

BRANDT, RICHARD. *Ethical Theory*. Englewood Cliffs, N.J.: Prentice-Hall, 1959.

CARRITT, E. F. *Morals and Politics*. Oxford: Clarendon, 1935.

————. *Ethical and Political Thinking*. Oxford: Clarendon, 1947.

————. *The Theory of Morals*. Oxford: Clarendon, 1952.

EWING, A. C. *The Individual, The State and World Government*. New York: Macmillan, 1947.

LAMONT, W. D. *The Principles of Moral Judgement*. Oxford: Clarendon, 1946.

MELDEN, A. I. *Rights and Right Conduct*. Oxford: Basil Blackwell, 1959.

6. Articles

BROWN, S. M., JR. "Inalienable Rights." *The Philosophical Review*, 64 (1955), 192-211.

FEINBERG, JOEL. "Duties, Rights and Claims." *American Philosophical Quarterly*, 3 (1966), 137-44.

FRANKENA, W. K. "Natural and Inalienable Rights." *The Philosophical Review*, 64 (1955), 212-32.

GOLDING, MARTIN. "Towards a Theory of Human Rights." *The Monist*, 4 (1968), 521-549.

HART, H. L. A. "Are There Any Natural Rights?" *The Philosophical Review*, 64 (1955), 175-191.

MACDONALD, MARGARET. "Natural Rights." *Philosophy, Politics and Society*. Ed. Peter Laslett. Oxford: Basil Blackwell, 1963.

MELDEN, A. I., and W. K. FRANKENA. "Symposium: The Concept of Universal Human Rights." *Science, Language and Human Rights*. Philadelphia: 1952, pp. 167-207.

STRAWSON, P. F. "Social Morality and Individual Ideal." *Philosophy*, 36 (1961), 1-17.

VLASTOS, GREGORY. "Justice and Equality." *Social Justice*. Ed. Richard Brandt. Englewood Cliffs, N.J.: Prentice-Hall, pp. 31-72.

WASSERSTROM, RICHARD. "Rights, Human Rights and Racial Discrimination." *Journal of Philosophy*, 61 (1964), 628-641.

WOLLHEIM, RICHARD. "Equality and Equal Rights." *Justice and Social Policy*. Ed. F. Olafson. Englewood Cliffs, N.J.: Prentice-Hall, 1961, pp. 111-127.

Index

187